W O
PH A

Period and Modern Architecture in Philadelphia
Tashka/Getty Images Plus

Getting to Philadelphia

By Air

Philadelphia International Airport – *8500 Essington Ave. (7 miles southwest of Center City)* - ✆ *(215) 937 6937 - www.phl.org.* **By car**, Center City is a 15 to 20-minute drive. Taxis *(fixed flat rate of $28.50)*, rental vehicles, group and private shuttles. Uber/VTC *(around $30)*.

Train: The **Airport Line** connects the terminals with several Center City stations including **Jefferson Station** *(Market Street between 10th and 12th St.)*, **Suburban Station** *(16th St. & JFK Boulevard)*, and the **main train station** (30th Street Station) *(www.septa.org - every 30 min. - 5am-midnight - $6.75).* It takes 30-35 min. to get to City Hall.

By Train

The train is a relatively fast and easy way to travel from New York to Philadelphia, a distance of about 80 miles. Take the **Amtrak** *(39 daily train services between the two cities)*, costing around $55 for a direct connection in 90 min. We recommend you book ahead as ticket prices can be steep if purchased on the day of travel. Depart from **Penn Station** *(33rd St. & 7th Ave. - Midtown Manhattan)*, set in a museum-worthy neoclassical colonnaded building dating from 1910, recently fully renovated. There is no direct access to the platform. Like at an airport, passengers with a ticket can relax in the waiting room until their train is called.

Amtrak: *www.amtrak.com.* If traveling from Washington-Baltimore *(1hr45 - from $53).* Tickets for trains with transfers cost less.

You come into Philadelphia at **30th Street Station** *(2955 Market St.)*, an imposing neoclassical and Art Deco structure (1933), very close to Center City. Catch a subway or trolley from the station on the corner of Market Street and S 33th St.

Best Port of Entry on the East Coast?

If you plan to visit multiple cities along the East Coast, it makes a lot of sense to enter the U.S. via Philadelphia. Its airport is far less busy than New York's, and boarding procedures are far speedier compared with other international airports. The transfer to Center City is fairly short and painless.

The Philadelphia Skyline.
benedek/Getty Images Plus

Unmissable
our selection of must-see sites

★★★ **Independence National Historical Park**
Map G5 - p. 24

★★★ **Barnes Foundation**
Map D4 - p. 51

★★★ **Philadelphia Museum of Art**
Map D3 - p. 53

★★ **Museum of the American Revolution**
Map G5 - p. 29

★ **Reading Terminal Mark**
Map F4 - p.

★★★ Benjamin Franklin Parkway
Map DE3-4 - p. 48

★★★ Nemours Estate
Map The Countryside - p. 67

Eastern State Penitentiary
Map D2-3 - p. 56

★★ Old City
Map G4-5 - p. 29

★★★ Winterthur Museum
Map The Countryside - p. 64

Our Top Picks

💜 **Browse the stalls of local producers at** Rittenhouse Square Farmers Market in Center City, or Headhouse Farmers Market in Old City. Take away fresh house-made products purchased from the variety of vendors. Or **wander around Cherry Street Pier,** a regenerated pier building turned hip mixed-use public space hosting artists, food trucks and market. See p. 35 and 97.

💜 **Go off, eyes peeled, in search of the countless murals—**huge wall paintings by artists and activists— dotted all over Philadelphia, one big open-air art museum. See p. 44.

💜 **Taste the star of local sandwiches, the famous Philly cheesesteak**: ribeye beef and melted cheese on a long bread roll. Head to one of the city's go-to cheesesteak destinations: Campo's in Old City or Ishkabibble's in funky South Street. See p. 75 and 76.

💜 **Ride your bike along the banks of Schuylkill River and enjoy the bucolic scenery of Fairmount Park**. An ideal spot to have a picnic or crack open a bottle and admire views of Boathouse Row, mock Tudor and Victorian rowing clubs, and rowers training with an elegance that makes it look effortless. See p. 14 and 62.

💜 **Get your fright on at the Halloween Nights at Eastern State Penitentiary**. If you visit Philadelphia between late September and early November, a tour of this creepy historic prison is highly recommended. Goosebumps guaranteed! See p. 56.

💜 **Catch some "art & R" in the Rodin Museum garden**. Free admission. A green oasis in the city. There's garden furniture to relax on and even a giant chessboard, although most visitors come to admire the outdoor sculptures from the museum's superb collection, such as *The Burghers of Calais*. See p. 53.

💜 **Watch and marvel at the Philadelphia Orchestra**, whose rich, powerful sounds and voluptuous timbres have made it one of the "Big Five", the top five symphony orchestras in the U.S. The cello-inspired performance venue at the Kimmel Cultural Campus has outstanding acoustics. See p. 99.

💜 **Attend a sporting event**, an essential vacation experience! From basketball to American football to baseball, Philadelphians are enthusiastic fans who live and breathe their teams. Is football more your game? You can relax: the city also has a soccer team, a finalist of the 2022 MLS championship. Not to mention that Philadelphia is one of the 16 host cities of the 2026 FIFA World Cup.

Cal Sport Media/Alamy/hemis.fr

The Philadelphia Eagles playing an American football match.

💜 **Brave the line to sup on the now TV-famous tacos at South Philly Barbacoa**, a restaurant that put chef Cristina Martinez on the culinary map and draws foodies from across the city and indeed the States! Everything from the tortillas to the tamarind juice is house-made, the flavors whisking diners away to Mexico. *See p. 81.*

💜 **Picture an artist's life on a visit to the studio of painter and illustrator Newell Convers Wyeth** at the Brandywine Museum of Art estate. In what resembles a large barn, boasting an impressive glass front where natural light floods in, the studio still has brushes, easels, and a handful of artworks to see. *See p. 65.*

💜 **Experience the magic of a musical** at the Walnut Street Theatre, the oldest such one in the U.S. (1809), or during a Broadway season at the Academy of Music, the country's oldest opera house (1857). There's no point going to New York when the shows here are Broadway quality and offer all the zest and virtuosity of the typical American production. Spellbinding! *See p. 56 and 98.*

Philadelphia in Five Days

Day 1

▶ Morning

The city boasts so much history that it's worth diving in right away. Head to the **Philadelphia Visitor Center Corporation** (*p. 24 and 117*) after first booking your tickets online for **Independence Hall★★**, the cradle of the American nation. Next catch a glimpse of the **Liberty Bell★★★** (*p. 27*), another American Revolution icon, before visiting the **National Constitution Center★★**, all about the U.S. Constitution (*p. 32*).

▶ Midday

How about lunch at **Reading Terminal Market★**, one of the oldest indoor markets in the U.S.? Choose from the tasty options offered by over 80 stalls and local producers, including members of Pennsylvania's Amish population (*p. 42*). For brunch or a quick snack, the pancakes at **Down Home Diner** (*p. 78*) are a treat.

▶ Afternoon

Delve deeper into America's history at the **Museum of the American Revolution★★** (*p. 29*), whose exhibits include the actual war tent used by George Washington. Explore Old City starting with a stroll around **Washington Square★** (*p. 43*) and the elegant streets lined with Georgian-style brick townhomes. Continue on to **Elfreth's Alley**, the nation's oldest continuously inhabited street (*p. 33*).

▶ Evening

Staying in history mode, board the **Moshulu**, a four-masted tall ship (1904) moored in the Penn's Landing Marina. A destination for cocktails, a romantic dinner, or both (*p. 76*).

Day 2

▶ Morning

History, check, now for the fine arts: head to the **Benjamin Franklin Parkway★★★**. To better appreciate the perspective, start at **City Hall★** (*p. 39*), designed to resemble the Hôtel de Ville in Paris but bigger and crowned with a monumental bell tower. It's then a short stroll to LOVE Park (*John F. Kennedy Plaza*), where taking a selfie or photo in front of the **LOVE sculpture** is the thing to do (*p. 49*). After reaching Logan Circle, see the Free Library, a carbon copy of the Hôtel Crillon in Paris. This is the start of the Benjamin Franklin Parkway which you can follow to the **Philadelphia Museum of Art★★★** (*p. 53*) and its rich collections that would take you more than a morning to fit in.

▶ Midday

Double back to Logan Circle to feast on local fare at **Urban Farmer** (*p. 81*).

▶ Afternoon

The **Barnes Foundation★★★** (*p. 51*) is the other must-see for art lovers. It has the finest Renoir and Cézanne collection in the world. Next, choose

DISCOVER THE
BEST DEALS
IN PHILADELPHIA

WE WELCOME YOU
WITH OPEN ARMS

Adventure Aquarium, C. Schultz

Eastern State Penitentiary, J. Fusco

between the **Rodin Museum★** *(p. 52)* or **Eastern State Penitentiary★★** *(p. 56)*, the world's first modern prison whose one-time inmates include Al Capone. If you opt for the Penitentiary, pop into the Rodin Museum garden, free to enter, for a quick rest.

▶ **Evening**

Head back to Old City for dinner at **Amada** *(p. 75)* on Chestnut Street, one of several Latin American eateries run by chef Jose Garces, a local star on the food scene.

Day 3

▶ **Morning**

Continue exploring the city with the fascinating collection at the **Mütter Museum★** *(p. 56)*. Or instead have fun tricking your eye at the **Museum of Illusions** *(p. 32)*.

▶ **Afternoon**

Tuck into Asian flavors in **Chinatown**, at **Dim Sum Garden** *(p. 79)* or **Penang** *(p. 79)*. Make room for dessert and other sweet treats, such as coconut tart or banana fritters at **Mayflower Café & Bakery** *(p. 92)*.

▶ **Afternoon**

Go for some retail therapy along the bustling shopping streets in the **South Philly** and **Queen Village** neighborhoods. With vintage thrift stores *(p. 97)*, uber-hip concept stores *(p. 96)*, tattoo parlors, barber's shops and organic markets, the area is colorful to say the least. Do your shopping then head to a cool coffee shop to soak up the local vibes. People love to chat in Philly, so don't be shy to strike up conversation with a neighbor.

▶ **Evening**

Continue your discovery of South Philadelphia in **Passyunk**. Have a drink at **Bok Bar** *(p. 92)*, an alternative venue with a rooftop occupying an old school. From there, admire the sunset over Philly's skyline. End the day with a taste of the Med at **Mish Mish** *(p. 81)*.

Day 4

▶ **Morning**

Time to explore the **Countryside of Philadelphia★**. Under an hour from Center City are lush rolling hills and stunning houses built by 19th century industrial magnates and contemporary artists who fell in love with the region. **Brandywine Valley** *(p. 63)* has an abundance of beautiful gardens which have earned it the title of "America's Garden Capital". Begin your tour with the first one: **Longwood Gardens★★**, the most lavish of them all with fountains, lakes and conservatories *(p. 63)*.

▶ **Midday**

The Winterthur Museum, Garden & Library is just 15 minutes away. Lunch at the museum's Visitor Center Café serving simple fare such as sandwiches, salads, and soup.

▶ **Afternoon**

Visit the **Winterthur Museum, Garden & Library★★★** *(p. 64)*, devoted to American decorative art in the former manor house of billionaire and philanthropist Henry Francis Du Pont. Jump in the car *(15 min.)* to another Du Pont family property: **Nemours**

imagoDens/Getty Images Plus

Abandoned corridor inside Eastern State Penitentiary.

Estate★★★ *(p. 67)*. This gem is an homage to French art and style.

▶ **Evening**

Take a trip to **West Chester** *(p. 68)*, a small historical city known for its colonial houses interspersed with neoclassical buildings. Stay at the **Warner Hotel** *(p. 104)*, and dine along the vibrant **Gay Street** lined with restaurants and shops.

Day 5

▶ **Morning**

Before quitting the Countryside, fans of big labels will want to go bargain-hunting at **Philadelphia Premium Outlets** *(p. 97)*, or shop till they drop at

King of Prussia Mall *(p. 97)*, one of the nation's largest malls. American history buffs will want to head to **Valley Forge National Historical Park** *(p. 70)*.

▶ **Lunch**

Back in Philly, stop for lunch in **University City** at **White Dog Cafe** *(p. 86)* where seasonal ingredients and local produce monopolize the menu. Or explore the history and flavors of the **Italian Market** on a food tour led by ebullient guide Jacquie. A professional chef and South Philly native with Italian roots, Jacquie—a font of knowledge on how waves of immigration have shaped the neighborhood—will have you taste local specialties while regaling you with stories *(p. 46)*.

▶Afternoon

If you plumped for University City, make a beeline for the **Penn Museum**, an archaeology and anthropology museum. It boasts well-documented collections, in particular on Native Americans, and is attached to the Ivy League University of Pennsylvania (p. 58).

▶Evening

Make your way to the fun and lively district of **Fishtown** (p. 37).

Walk up Frankford Avenue to check out its vintage and record stores before exploring the tequila and mezcal menu for cocktail hour at **LMNO** (p. 77). Then dine at **Suraya** (p. 78) for a taste of the Levant. Cap off your trip in style at one of Philly's various jazz clubs, such as **South** (p. 99) or **Time** (p. 98).

R. Duchaine/Alamy/hemis.fr

Philadelphia's Rodin Museum.

Beauty Every Day

Experience dazzling displays, performances that inspire, majestic fountains, and a place to relax and reconnect with nature. Longwood Gardens is nestled in the heart of the Brandywine Valley outside Philadelphia.

LONGWOOD
GARDENS

longwoodgardens.org

Philly by Bike

Cycling makes a great way to explore Philadelphia—a mostly flat city that is relatively compact. Plus, it's easy to find your bearings, Old City has narrow lanes and so less traffic, and Philly is blessed with over 180 miles of bike paths.

While there are plenty of cycle routes to choose from (*see box*), the one we recommend below hugs the winding Schuylkill River and is protected. Perfect for a family day out.

Schuylkill River Trail

😊 *The trail makes a loop in Fairmount Park (8.5 miles). Caution: The trail is not reserved exclusively for cyclists so be mindful of pedestrians and runners.*

▶ Start: 9/11 Memorial on Schuylkill Banks

There are multiple access points to the bike trail following the riverbank. If you enter at the **9/11 Memorial** (in memory of the September 11 attacks), near **Chestnut Street** and its eponymous bridge, a section of the trail is urban, taking you between river and railway. A short ride northwards later and, on the opposite bank, the grand **30th Street Station**, a mix of neoclassical and Art Deco, comes into view. In the vicinity of Paine's Park, look out on your right for the **Philadelphia Museum of Art**, marking the gateway to Fairmount Park.

▶ Stop 1: Fairmount Water Works

This waterworks, which supplied Philadelphia with water from 1815

to 1909, is worth a stop to admire its stunning buildings with Greek Revival colonnades.

▶ Stop 2: Boathouse Row

This row of mock Tudor and Victorian boathouses and rowing clubs from the 19th c. appears quintessentially British (*p. 60*).

▶ Stop 3: Statue of John B. Kelly

Why is there a statue of the father of Grace Kelly (*p. 136*) rowing? Because he was triple Olympic rowing champion from 1920 to 1924. Watching rowers train on the river is one of this trail's highlights.

▶ Stop 4: Laurel Hill Cemetery

A few wheel spins after crossing Strawberry Mansion Bridge, Laurel

Indego

Stations in Philly's official bike share program are dotted over the city (*see p. 117 and www.rideindego.com*).

Sites with itineraries

discoverphl.com: This site has a "Guide to Biking in Philadelphia" and suggested itineraries.

schuylkillriver.org/map In the north section, cyclists can extend the Schuylkill River Trail by 30 miles to Valley Forge.

www.delawareriverwaterfront. com/places/delaware-river-trail1: A scenic 3-mile trail along the Delaware River, from Pier 70 in South Philadelphia to Penn Treaty Park, in Fishtown.

Cyclists in Philadelphia.

Hill Cemetery will come into view on your right. The site boasts beautiful landscaping and monumental burial plots. The highest point of the cemetery affords superb river views. *Pay attention crossing this busy road.* Continue on to **Falls Bridge**, a steel Pratt truss bridge that takes you to the opposite bank. Stay on the same stretch when you ride off the bridge. The bike lane is narrower, squeezed between river and road, but it is protected. Follow Martin Luther King Junior Drive for nearly 4 miles.

▶ **Stop 5 : Fairmount Fish Ladder**
While a fish ladder may well float your boat, most cyclists stop here to enjoy the view. The ideal spot to take a photo of Boathouse Row on the other bank, and Fairmount Weir from where you can make out the Philadelphia Museum of Art and its neoclassical façade dominating the river.
Continue on the same road, which crosses to the other bank via Martin Luther King Junior Drive Bridge. Once over the bridge, veer right to go back down the bike trail hugging the river: **Schuylkill Banks**. On your return to Center City, take in the breathtaking Philly skyline.

A Word from the Greeters: I Love Philly!

Steve Weinik

Jane Golden.

Jane Golden, founder and executive director of Mural Arts Philadelphia

I was born in Minnesota and raised in New Jersey. After graduating from Stanford University with a double major in fine art and political science, I moved to Los Angeles to become a painter and mural artist. Then in 1983, I returned to join my family on the East Coast. A year later, the Mayor of Philadelphia's office contacted me and asked me to run the Anti-Graffiti Network. I hoped to transform the image of graffiti artists from anti-establishment to engaged and useful members of the community. This laid the foundation of Mural Arts Philadelphia.

Given a chance to improve my adopted city through art, include both officials and unknowns in art projects, bring meaning to the lives of young people from complex backgrounds, and change mentalities, I instantly realized that my life would be in Philadelphia. It's a love story that has continued for 38 years!

Your favorite place in Philadelphia?
My neighborhood, near the **Museum of Art** and Barnes Foundation, on the river. It's peaceful and people like to walk their dogs there–I think my dog would agree!

And your favorite place to eat?
Parc, across from **Rittenhouse Square**. Their French onion soup is delicious, and the terrace is the perfect spot for people-watching.

Three good reasons to live in Philadelphia?
1. The art. It has museums, cultural centers, murals, public art, everyone has access to art; no neighborhood is left out.
2. Our parks and gardens with greenery, fresh air, and outdoor activities for everyone.
3. Our diversity! Philly's history, multiculturalism, colors, aromas... Our murals vouch for it: Philadelphia is an incredible patchwork!

Yannick Nézet-Séguin, Music Director of the Philadelphia Orchestra

I love Philadelphia! The city reminds me of my hometown of Montreal. It's a very neighborhood-focused city. It's also very walkable, with beautiful old buildings everywhere you look. I love the originality of Philadelphia's food and arts scenes—truly some of the best food and art in the world comes out of Philadelphia kitchens and venues. Philly residents are outgoing and welcoming, like our wonderful neighbors in **Washington Square** where my husband, Pierre, and I recently moved to. It's conveniently located near the **Kimmel Center** (performing arts venue), and we've enjoyed all of the beautiful outdoor spaces, amazing restaurants, and great shopping,

Your favorite place to walk in Philadelphia?

I'm very active and dedicated to my fitness routine. The **Schuylkill River** and **Fairmount Park** are among my favorite outdoor spaces.

Your favorite place to have a drink?

For a great cappuccino, a great cocktail on a sunny afternoon, or a nice bottle of champagne to celebrate a great concert, my favorite place is **Rittenhouse Square.** I love to immerse myself in the beautiful atmosphere of this gorgeous area.

Three good reasons to live in Philadelphia?

1. The incredibly rich and diverse arts and culture scene. From classical to jazz, hip hop to opera, fine art to theater..., Philadelphia has it all.
2. I like to think that food is a symphony for the senses, and we have many talented maestros in this city. The dining options are unmatched.
3. The people! I love connecting with audiences and feeling the deep sense of hometown pride that all Philadelphians share (me included).

Pete Checcha/Philadelphia Orchestra

Yannick Nézet-Séguin.

17

Chef Michael Solomonov.

Chef Michael Solomonov, co-owner of restaurants Zahav, K'far Cafe and Laser Wolf

I was born in Israel and grew up in Pittsburgh, Pennsylvania's other big city. I went back to Israel then returned to study at the Florida Culinary Institute. Much younger, I was en route for New York dreaming of opening my own restaurant when I made a pitstop in Philadelphia. I immediately fell in love with the place: its history, its more modern side, its fusions, its cosmopolitan atmosphere that can also be found on the culinary scene and so on our plates! I didn't need any more convincing to stay in Philadelphia.
I moved here and never left.

I've found my balance in Philadelphia. Living here makes you open up to others and become a better person. There's a sense of community here, pride in our accomplishments, openness and a willingness to listen, values close to my heart that I strive to live by every day with my family, my kitchen teams, and the diners at my restaurant Zahav. I want everyone to enjoy their dining experience, breaking bread together around hearty Israeli cuisine offering delicate, mouthwatering flavors, in the heart of Philly's Old City.

Your favorite place in Philadelphia?
I walk a lot and I love the charm of **Society Hill**, a neighborhood next to Old City. The period houses along the peaceful, leafy cobbled streets both take me back to another time and soothe the soul.

And your favorite place to eat?
Without hesitation, **Royal Sushi & Izakaya**, in the Queen Village district.

Three good reasons to live in Philadelphia?
1. Its museums and art events. It's just as good as New York in terms of cultural venues and programming.

2. The freedom it offers on a personal level, to express oneself and realize your dreams. The city is historic but progressive.

3. Philly has many faces and that's where its magic lies. It's at once Liberty Bell, the Declaration of Independence and... Rocky Balboa! *(laughs)*

Fareed Simpson, trumpeter and professor of music at Temple University

I was born and bred in Philly, as Philadelphia is affectionately called! My family, friendly and professional ties are all here. I still live here, teaching music and playing in the clubs.

I love its inimitable atmosphere where, although each area is different, everyone feels good and loves to connect with others, whatever the neighborhood. Philadelphia has a strong human identity; we're proud of our city and our history that is inextricably linked with our national history. We also take immense pride in our spirit of cooperation and community, our sports teams, and our local talents, be they entrepreneurs, artists, restaurateurs, chefs, or... musicians!

Your favorite place in Philadelphia?
Center City, what we call our downtown. The place has an energy and population mix that has created incredible cultural diversity. That's the essence of Philly you feel, whether you live here or are just passing through. I love its architecture, which ranges from historic buildings to towers of glass and steel. I also love its parks in the city or on the river, leafy streets and murals, genuine works of art accessible to everyone, which make it unique. You have to try the hip restaurants, rooftop bars and clubs: evenings in Center City are fun!

Your favorite place to have a drink?
South for food and drinks while listening to live jazz.

Three good reasons to live in Philadelphia?
1. The food scene: there is so much variety, for every preference, pocket, and taste.

2. Since I come from a family of musicians, started to play trumpet aged 8, and am a great fan of John Coltrane, a Philly native, I obviously have to say the music and arts scene—simply incredible.

3. Our sports teams and fans. We are loyal to our athletes and the concept of fair play. There's no atmosphere like it!

19

Temple University

Fareed Simpson.

VISIT PHILADELPHIA

Statue of William Penn by Alexander Milne Calder.
Mindaugas Dulinskas/Getty Images Plus

Philadelphia Today

Set along the Delaware River, between frantic New York and lofty Washington, about 100 miles from one and 150 miles from the other, Philadelphia is the little sister unfairly snubbed by tourists. Yet it offers the perfect compromise between American excess and European spirit, not to mention all the appeal of a city packed with art, history, and a cultural effervescence few people expect.

America's Most Historic Square Mile

Philadelphia is blessed with an aristocratic charm imparted by long-established dynasties and can boast a glorious past, not least owing to its role as the U.S. capital for almost a decade, from 1790 to 1799. It was also the American financial center for just under 40 years, from 1790. It was here that the most famous chapters of the American Revolution were written: **Independence National Historical Park** and the **Old City** district are regarded as "the Most Historic Square Mile" in America, and Philadelphia the first city in the United States to be inscribed on the **UNESCO World Heritage List.** A history in which the names Washington, Franklin, La Fayette, and Jefferson are key protagonists.

The "Frenchest" American City

While the sixth-largest city in the United States is typically American for its skyline, wide boulevards, and grid street plan, Philadelphia is an incredibly manageable city where you can easily get around on foot. Tourists will love exploring the city on foot—and may do a double take when casting their eyes on certain buildings: **City Hall**, almost completely identical to the Hôtel de Ville in Paris; the **Free Library** and **Municipal Court**, near-perfect facsimiles of the Crillon and La Marine hotels respectively, on Paris' Place de la Concorde; the **Rodin Museum**, the second-largest in the world, after Paris; and even an equestrian **statue of Joan of Arc** by French sculptor Frémiet.

Arty Philly: A Legacy of Beauty

Few North American cities have shown such consideration to art and urban planning. "Philly", as the city is affectionately called, is practically an open-air museum. Everywhere you look are statues, porticos, Greek Revival or neoclassical pediments, museums... The **Benjamin Franklin Parkway**, inspired by the Champs-Élysées in Paris, was built to restore Philadelphia's natural and artistic beauty. It is lined with illustrious museums including the **Philadelphia Museum of Art,** one of the nation's largest art museums, and the **Barnes Foundation**, home to the biggest collection of artworks by Renoir and Cézanne in the world.

22

Rocky, Renaissance Personified

Much like Detroit and Baltimore, Philadelphia didn't escape the effects of deindustrialization that pummeled the major cities on the East Coast. From the 1950s, the city's factories upped sticks, leading to a social, economic, and demographic crisis that sent one-third of Philly's population away in 30 years. While the 1970s could be described as Philadelphia's darkest period, in recent years the trend has reversed, despite the Great Recession of 2008 and the COVID-19 pandemic. The **Rocky** franchise, incarnated by Sylvester Stallone, has continued for almost 40 years and symbolizes the city's renewal: an Italian-American from the ghetto overcoming life's obstacles in the 1970s to become a champion boxer. A metaphor that has transformed Philly's image and put it on the world stage. Don't leave without taking the obligatory selfie in front of the **Rocky** statue.

Philadelphia is a global medical hub, not surprising given its established hospitals and medical faculties—and that Benjamin Franklin set up the country's first hospital and university here. Over 40 companies locally are involved in cell and gene therapy research. America's leading cable operator Comcast has its headquarters in Philadelphia, which is a major business services center—in the insurance, transportation, and banking sectors—, another legacy from the past.

The New American Revolution

This economic revival was complemented by an urban and social renaissance, surfing on the wave of rooftop bars, farmers markets, vintage stores, craft breweries, and distilleries. But in the cheesesteak capital, the revolution that really counts is food-driven. Philly is home to some of the best chefs on the East Coast, from Jose Garces (restaurant **Amada**) to Michael Solomonov (**Zahav**), and more recently Cristina Martinez (**South Philly Barbacoa** and **Casa Mexico**), three winners of the much-coveted James Beard Award. Among the rising stars, the young Amanda Shulman draws those in the know to **Her Place Supper Club** while the firm favorites are Greg Vernick and Jean-Georges Vongerichten, whose restaurant on the 59th story of the Four Seasons Hotel is a pinnacle, in every sense, affording the most spectacular views of Philly and America you can only dream of!

Multicultural and Cool Philadelphia

Philadelphia is a city of two halves: traditional but also hip, multicultural, and tolerant, with its murals (over 4,000), and poor neighborhoods too, although gentrification is happening. Like **Fishtown**, the one-time industrial district, now hipster central thanks to its cooler-than-cool bars, art galleries, and gig venues, drawing in crowds to dance to the small hours. Philadelphia, the "City of Brotherly Love", welcomes you with open arms.

Old City ★★
Society Hill ★
and Penn's Landing

The cradle of American history, the "City of Brotherly Love" founded by William Penn symbolizes the first steps taken by the young American nation. A history thankfully well preserved in the city's historic districts: Independence National Historical Park and Old City. Tread on the deep roots of American democracy as you explore its quaint streets and visit its abundance of museums. History also awaits you in the residential neighborhood of Society Hill which boasts a handful of historic monuments and streets bordered by period brick houses and where some lanes still have their original cobblestones. On fine days, walk as far as Penn's Landing, the now regenerated former docklands on the Delaware River.

▶ **Getting there:** Ⓜ 5th St. Independence Hall Station or Market St. & 2nd St. on the Market-Frankford Line. If your lodgings are not too far in the suburbs, you can easily get around on foot. This is in fact true for every area covered by this guide.

Local Map p. 26. Detachable Map GH3-6.

▶ **Tip:** Make a beeline for the Visitor Center for information. Set aside at least a day to explore these two history-rich areas, but don't expect to see it all.

INDEPENDENCE NATIONAL HISTORICAL PARK ★★★

G5 ☏ (215) 965 2305 - www.nps.gov/inde/index.htm - unless indicated otherwise, sites are open 9am-5pm - admission free.

Bordered east and west by 2nd St. and 6th St., and north and south by Market St. and Walnut St., the historic park spanning more than 51 acres was created to preserve several monuments that were already standing during the tumultuous period when the United States was founded. It proudly houses the most esteemed symbols of liberty in the country: Independence Hall and The Liberty Bell.

☺ There is a limited number of tickets for Independence Hall for each time slot. You can book in advance on the park's website (www.nps.gov/inde/index.htm - $1 booking fee).

Liberty Bell Center ★★

G5 526 Market St., between 5th St. and 6th St.

The modern, glass-fronted building across from Independence Hall

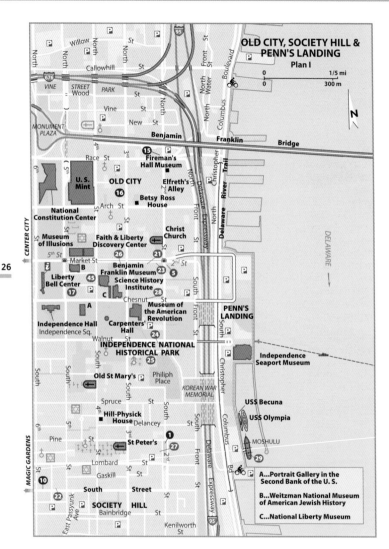

OLD CITY, SOCIETY HILL &
PENN'S LANDING
Plan I

0   1/5 mi
0   300 m

N

Willow St
North
North St
Callowhill St
VINE
STREET Wood PARK
Vine St
New St
MONUMENT PLAZA
Benjamin Franklin Bridge
CENTER CITY

Race St
Fireman's Hall Museum 15
OLD CITY 16
Elfreth's Alley
Betsy Ross House
Arch St
National Constitution Center
Museum of Illusions
Faith & Liberty Discovery Center 26
Christ Church
21
Market St
Benjamin Franklin Museum
Liberty Bell Center 17
Science History Institute 28
23 5
Chestnut St
Museum of the American Revolution 24
Independence Hall
Independence Sq.
Carpenters' Hall
Walnut St
INDEPENDENCE NATIONAL HISTORICAL PARK 25
Old St Mary's
Philiph Place
KOREAN WAR MEMORIAL
Spruce St
Hill-Physick House
Delancey
St Peter's 1 27
Pine St
Lombard St
Gaskill St
South Street
SOCIETY HILL
Bainbridge St
Kenilworth St
East Passyunk Ave
22
MAGIC GARDENS
10

U.S. Mint

North Water
Columbus Boulevard
Front St
North

Delaware River Trail
Christopher
Delaware Expressway
North 2nd St
Front St
South

PENN'S LANDING

DELAWARE

Independence Seaport Museum

USS Becuna
USS Olympia

MOSHULU
29

Christopher
Columbus Bd
Delaware Expressway

A...Portrait Gallery in the
Second Bank of the U.S.

B...Weitzman National Museum
of American Jewish History

C...National Liberty Museum

zealously guards the revered **Liberty Bell★★★**. Cast in London, it had to be recast soon after arriving in Philadelphia when its rim cracked upon the first strike. It was placed in the steeple of what is now Independence Hall in 1753 where it stayed for nearly 100 years. The bell, engraved with a verse from the Book of Leviticus (Old Testament) proclaiming "LIBERTY Throughout all the Land unto all the Inhabitants Thereof", was rung to mark the first reading of the Declaration of Independence, on July 8, 1776. In the 19th century, slavery abolitionists renamed it "Liberty Bell". Today, Liberty Bell stands as an iconic symbol of freedom.

Independence Hall ★★

G5 *520 Chestnut St., between 5th St. and 6th St.*

Now a UNESCO World Heritage Site, the Georgian brick building featuring a dome (1748) was, originally, the seat of government of Pennsylvania. In May 1775, the delegates from the Thirteen Colonies held the Second Continental Congress meeting in the Assembly Room to agree on a

A Citizen Second to None

The fifteenth child of a British soap manufacturer who emigrated to Boston in the early 18th century, **Benjamin Franklin** (1706-1790) only completed two years at school before he was apprenticed to his brother James in 1718. At age 17, Franklin ran away to Philadelphia where he eventually set up his own printing shop. Exploring his creative side, in 1732 he published, under the pseudonym Richard Saunders, *Poor Richard's Almanach*, "sermons" intended to instruct the public. He became an influential Philadelphia citizen, establishing numerous institutions such as the Library of Philadelphia, the Pennsylvania Hospital, and the Academy of Philadelphia, the forerunner to the University of Pennsylvania. Franklin simultaneously pursued his passion for science and his experiments with electricity earned him European celebrity. Elected to the Colonial Assembly in 1751, he devoted much of his life to politics and fighting for independence. While Benjamin Franklin is revered in the United States as one of the Founding Fathers, the people of Philadelphia proudly call him a citizen "second to none".

response to the growing aggression from the British. **George Washington** was appointed Commander in Chief of the Continental Army in late summer, which King George III interpreted as an open act of rebellion. The Declaration of Independence was unanimously adopted on July 4, 1776, signaling the official start of the American War of Independence. People gathered on **Independence Square** on July 8, 1776, to hear the first public reading of the Declaration. In 1781, while secession seemed imminent, Independence Hall was the place where the Articles of Confederation were ratified. Six years later, the Constitutional Convention appointed a government and, in 1788, the Constitution was passed by a majority of states. The building has reclaimed its 1776 appearance and most of its original paneling has survived.

On either side of the building stand **Congress Hall** (west), the meeting place of the House of Representatives and the Senate of the new American nation (1790-1800), and **Old City Hall**★ (east) where the Supreme Court sat from 1791 to 1800.

American Philosophical Society – *104 S. 5th St. - ☎ (215) 440 3400 - www.amphilsoc.org - Tue-Sun 10am-4pm; summer: 10am-5pm - admission free.* The members of this institution founded by **Benjamin Franklin** in 1743 continue to assemble here today. It also hosts temporary exhibitions on historical subjects.

Library Hall – *105 S. 5th St. - ☎ (215) 440 3400 - www.amphilsoc.org - Mon-Fri 9am-4:30pm - admission free.* This library also established by Benjamin Franklin could be described as the ancestor of the Library of Congress. It houses over 350,000 volumes and periodicals, 11 million manuscripts, 250,000 images, and an incalculable number of originals, a large proportion of which can be viewed online.

Portrait Gallery in the Second Bank of the United States ★ (A)

G5 *420 Chestnut St. - www.nps.gov - May-Sep: 10am-5pm; rest of year: check the website.*
This marble-columned building (1818, William Strickland) is a fine example of Greek Revival architecture. Opened in 1824, the bank was one of the most powerful financial institutions in the world until President Andrew Jackson repealed its charter (1832). The site now hosts a collection of portraits of key figures from American history.

Carpenters' Hall

G5 *320 Chestnut St. - ☎ (215) 925 0167 - www.carpentershall.org - Tue-Sun, 10am-4pm - closed on Tue in Jan-Feb.*
In a Georgian style, this red brick building with white moldings (1770) has belonged to the Carpenters' Guild of Philadelphia since day one. In 1774, the 56 delegates from the Thirteen Colonies, revolted by the "intolerable

laws" inflicted by Great Britain, met for the first time here (First Continental Congress) to consider how to react. Visitors can now admire objects on display from that period, including documents, furniture, paintings, and flags.

Benjamin Franklin Museum (Franklin Court) ★

G5 *Entrance on Market St. or Chestnut St., between 3rd St. and 4th St. - Museum: 9am-5pm - $5 (ages 4-16 $2).*
One of Philadelphia's most esteemed former residents *(see box p. 27)*, Benjamin Franklin built the family home here, in 1760. A steel structure now outlines the spot where the house once stood. The **Benjamin Franklin Museum★** is cleverly organized around the life and work of this extraordinary figure. The **Printing Office** highlights the pivotal role of the press and the circulation of news, which Franklin was one of the first to support. The newspaper office he made for his grandson, Benjamin Franklin Bache, printer and newspaper publisher, has been reconstructed *(demonstrations of the machinery take place several times daily)*.
At the far north side of Franklin Court, the **Market Street Houses**, reconstructions of townhouses built by Benjamin Franklin in the 1780s, feature working reproductions of the original print shop and bindery.
In the vicinity are other sites not strictly part of the historic park but worth a visit if you have time.

OLD CITY ★★

ℹ️ *www.oldcitydistrict.org.*
The area where William Penn first settled, this district, bound by Florist St. in the north, Walnut St. south, 6th St. west and the Delaware River east, has seen a spectacular renaissance. Worlds apart from the state of abandon the area was in just decades earlier. Hip restaurants and restored historic buildings—now premises for theater troops, artist studios, and art galleries—line the streets of this neighborhood where visitors will also find a good number of original shops and more traditional places to eat.
Free Quaker Meeting House – *Corner of 5th St. and Arch St.* Dating from 1783, it symbolizes the strong Quaker presence during Philadelphia's early days.
😊 On the first Friday of the month, local galleries, exhibition venues, and theaters stay open late (5pm-9pm).

Museum of the American Revolution ★★

G5 *101 S. 3rd St. - ☏ (215) 253 6731 - www.amrevmuseum.org - 10am-5pm - $25 without booking or $21 if timeslot reserved; combined ticket with the National Constitution Center $29.*
Devoted to the war that led to the birth of the American nation, this excellent museum provides a brilliant introduction to this founding chapter of history and the sites linked to it. It features a collection of exhibits seldom or never seen before: weapons, papers,

miscellaneous objects, suits and uniforms, paintings, and the most priceless relic from the time, the actual **campaign tent** used by George Washington★★★. This is "staged" in its own room which you can enter following a film screening (shown hourly).

Visitors are guided, in chronological order, through the stages of the war in the American colonies fought in the late 18th century and explanations are given on the protagonists, the issues at stake, and the contradictions—where did women and slaves sit within this struggle for freedom? Visit highlights: the statue of King George III toppled in New York in 1776, the Battle of Brandywine (**C** p. 67) as if you were there, and the true-to-life reproduction of the Liberty Tree that stood in Boston where "the sons and daughters of liberty" gathered to show their defiance.

Weitzman National Museum of American Jewish History ★ (B)

G5 101 S. Independence Mall - ✆ (215) 923 3811 - www.theweitzman.org - Fri-Sun, 10am-5 pm - free thanks to the Jane and Daniel Och Family Foundation.

One of the latest additions to Philly's plethora of museums, this striking glass-fronted museum tells the 360-year history of Jewish people in the U.S. The chronological experience begins on the top floor, where visitors start their journey through time that is interactive, living, and "made flesh" as almost every chapter is told through true events. History with a capital H is interspersed with dozens of personal accounts: a chance to explore the everyday life and traditions of this diverse diaspora. The **Hall of Fame** on the first floor concludes the visit, featuring portraits of American Jewish celebrities, such as the politician Golda Meir, the singer Barbra Streisand, the film director Steven Spielberg, and the writer Isaac B. Singer.

Faith & Liberty Discovery Center ★

G5 101 N. Independence Mall East - ✆ (215) 309 0401 - www.faithandliberty.org - Mon-Sat, 10am-5pm - $10 (ages 7-17 $8). You receive an interactive lamp at the entrance which activates the exhibits you want to learn more about as you go around. You are also given a lamp number so you can further explore at home any digital assets you collected during your visit, an interesting way to extend the experience. Opened in 2021 by the **American Bible Society**, this is the latest addition to Philadelphia's museum collection. This immersive museum invites visitors to explore the relationship between faith and liberty from the founding of the **United States** through today. The interactive exhibits shine a light on the Bible's influence on people at historic and personal milestones through the lens of faith, liberty, justice, and hope. From the first Quakers who arrived in America to

Museum of the American Revolution

"Who, that was not a witness, could imagine that...
men who came from the different parts of the continent,
strongly disposed...to despise and quarrel with each other,
would instantly become but one patriotic band of brothers."

GEORGE WASHINGTON,
FAREWELL ORDERS TO THE CONTINENTAL A
NOVEMBER 2, 1783

"Savage-looking riflemen"

live their faith freely to confrontations with the Native Americans and the subject of slavery, you are taken through every combat waged in the name of liberty by different groups, including abolitionists, suffragettes, and civil rights activists. Perhaps more compelling than the accounts of great historical figures like Abraham Lincoln or Martin Luther King are the testimonials of countless unknown Americans: refugees, soldiers returning from Iraq or Afghanistan, victims of 9/11, and others.

Museum of Illusions

G5 *401 Market Street - ☎ (267) 703 2270 - moiphilly.com - daily 10am-8:30pm - $23 (ages 5-12 $18) - online booking advised.*

The entertaining Museum of Illusions is highly recommended for families traveling with kids or anyone who's a kid at heart! Visitors get to explore the fascinating world of sensory illusions—visual, auditory, and dimensional. The immersive and interactive experience is made up of various spaces and galleries where the illusions are more mind-bending from one to the next. For each trick of the eye, visitors are totally immersed in the scene and become truly part of the illusion. A fun and educational way to learn why our senses perceive things our brain cannot understand. Given how eye-catching the exhibits are, unsurprisingly this museum ranks among the most Insta-worthy spots in Philadelphia, so cameras at the ready for those selfies!

National Constitution Center ★★

G4 *525 Arch St. - ☎ (215) 409 6600 - constitutioncenter.org - Wed-Sun, 10am-5pm - $14.50.*

Fitting in with other sites in the area, this ultra-modern building houses a one-of-a-kind center. It is devoted to the **American Constitution**, ratified in Independence Hall in 1788 and in operation since 1789. It is the museum of "We the People", the first line of the Constitution, a document that continues to hold significant importance in the eyes of American citizens. Exhibits include films, interactive questionnaires, and interesting artefacts. Test out your knowledge of American history and set eyes on a host of iconic objects: President Roosevelt's fedora, the gown worn by Justice O'Connor, the first woman named to the Supreme Court, in 1981, a print of the Constitution that appeared in a local newspaper over 200 years ago, and many more.

United States Mint

G4 *151 N. Independence Mall E. - ☎ (215) 408 0112 - www.usmint.gov - check for opening hours - free - photo ID required to enter.*

The first mint in America was established in Philadelphia in 1792. It was moved three times before it found its current home, in 1969, in the building open to visitors today, regarded as the largest structure of its kind worldwide. Learn all the secrets of how coins are manufactured, a process you can see in action from a footbridge a dozen meters above the production line. As meticulous as it all appears, the facility manages to produce a million coins every half hour! See the first American coin press (1792) and meet Peter, a bald eagle which inhabited the first building. Don't miss a chance to admire the glass mosaics made by Tiffany (1901) for the inauguration of the third building and reinstalled here. The panels illustrate the ancient Roman process of coinage.

Christ Church ★

G5 *2ⁿᵈ St., north of Market St. - ☏ (215) 922 1695 - www.christchurchphila.org - daily 11am-5pm - $5 (children $2).*
Founded in 1695 as a parish of the Church of England, Christ Church is a fine example of Georgian architecture (1754) surmounted by a tower. The church's royalist congregation switched camps when George Washington and 15 signatories of the Declaration of Independence attended to their religious duties there. It is regarded by many as a "church of the nation". William Penn was baptized as an Anglican there in the **baptismal font**, located in the rear of the church and brought over from England.
Christ Church Burial Ground – *Corner of N. 5ᵗʰ St. and Arch St. - summer: Wed-Sun, 12pm-4pm, Mar-Dec (weather permitting) - $5 (ages 5-12 $2).* A few blocks from the church, the cemetery is the resting place of notable citizens such as Benjamin Franklin along with numerous Revolutionary War heroes

and signatories of the Declaration of Independence.

Elfreth's Alley ★

G4 *Between N. 2ⁿᵈ St. and Front St.*
This quaint street established in the 18th century was named after its owner, blacksmith Jeremiah Elfreth. Some houses date from 1725. Its former tenants of tradespeople and artisans are long gone, having made way for today's privileged citizens who can lay claim to live on "the nation's oldest continuously inhabited street".
Elfreth's Alley Museum – *No. 126 - ☏ (215) 574 0560 - www.elfrethsalley. org - times vary, enquire - $3 (ages 7-12 $2).* Occupying a tailor's house, the museum offers a snapshot of everyday life in colonial times.

Betsy Ross House

G4 *239 Arch St. - ☏ (215) 629 4026 - historicphiladelphia.org - 10am-5pm - $8 (children $6).*
This brick building is said to be where Quaker seamstress **Betsy Ross** (1752-1836) lived when she sewed the first Star-Spangled Banner. Her lodging and workshop have been well preserved. The landmark hosts temporary exhibitions on historical themes and activities for all ages (film screenings, cooking workshops, etc.).

National Liberty Museum (C)

G5 *321 Chestnut Street - ☏ (215) 925 2800 - www.libertymuseum. org - Thu-Mon, 10am-5pm - $12 (ages 6-17 $6, over 65s $10).*

When the museum was officially opened in 2000, its founder declared: "We who are fortunate enough to live in the land of liberty must protect it, preserve it, and guard it for future generations." The museum is educational in nature, dedicated to strengthening the basic principles for safeguarding liberty, including heroism, empathy, and the appreciation of diversity. The exhibit on the heroes of liberty is particularly touching, from the replica of Nelson Mandela's cell on Robben Island to the annex where Anne Frank was hidden, not to mention photos of firefighters who lost their lives during the September 11 attacks in 2001.

Science History Institute

G5 315 Chestnut Street - ℘ (215) 925 2222 - www.sciencehistory.org - Wed-Sat, 10am-5pm - admission free.
Science is all around us. It shapes who we are and what we do—from the clothing we wear to the food we eat to the water we drink. Yet how science influences our lives often goes unremarked. The purpose of this museum is to put hidden technology and the history of science's successes, failures, and surprises it has given us, under the microscope. It presents a concise overview of the evolution of science and chemistry in a way that helps non-scientists understand the progress made. Various everyday objects—from LED bulbs to plastic bottles–give up their secrets.

Fireman's Hall Museum

G4 147 N. 2nd St. - ℘ (215) 923 1438 - www.firemanshallmuseum.org - Tue-Sat, 10am-4pm - admission free.
This museum housed in a fire station from 1902 explores humankind's ongoing battle with fire, a scourge on wooden cities in the past. Uniforms, trucks, apparatus, photos, and more are on display. It's the oldest fire museum in the U.S.

PENN'S LANDING AND SOCIETY HILL ★

Fronting the Delaware River, just east of Old City, lies **Penn's Landing** where William Penn and the first colonists landed and took shelter in caves hollowed into the cliffs. The district between Vine Street and South Street has been turned into a recreation area with running paths, ice-skating rink, amphitheater, and seaport museum. The northern end is dominated by the **Benjamin Franklin Bridge**, spanning the Delaware River, while the southern end is where you'll find the hip restaurants and clubs of South Street. Springing up during the turbulent years preceding America's independence, 18th-century churches and houses gracefully line the streets of **Society Hill**, a district abutting Penn's Landing and bound by Independence Hall and Lombard Street. Some of the city's most beautiful churches, restored, are concentrated in historic Society Hill.

VisionsbyAtlee/Getty Images Plus

Society Hill in Old City.

Among them, **St Peter's** *(313 Pine St.)* dates from 1761, **Old St Mary's** *(252 St. 4th St.)* was erected in 1763, and **Gloria Dei Church/Old Swedes Church**★ *(916, S. Swanson St.)*, the oldest church in Philadelphia, was founded around 1700 by Lutherans from Sweden.
Cherry Street Pier – *121 N. Christopher Columbus Blvd - www.cherrystreetpier. com.* A testament to the city's successful regeneration, this municipal pier building and loading dock on the riverbank now houses artist residencies, a farmers market, an open-air garden, food trucks, and various exhibition spaces.

Independence Seaport Museum ★

G5 *211 S. Columbus Blvd (pedestrian entrance via the Walnut St. bridge) - ℘ (215) 413 8655 - www.phillyseaport. org - daily 10am-5pm - $18 (children $14).*

This expansive museum on the Delaware River's banks puts on temporary exhibitions on maritime history, trade, and immigration, sectors that contributed to the port's development. Two historic United States ships are anchored close by: the **USS Olympia**★, the flagship cruiser of Admiral Dewey (1892), the

Edgar Allan Poe National Historical Site

Edgar Allan Poe (1809-1849), writer of short stories and novels, poet, and playwright, is one of America's most famous authors. He is generally regarded to have penned the first detective, science fiction and fantasy novels. Poe lived in Philadelphia from 1838 to 1844. These six years were said to be the happiest of his life, although in **1842** his wife Virginia **contracted tuberculosis. Illness and financial woes plunged Poe into a period of deep depression. A period** that was also his most prolific; in Philadelphia, Poe published his best-known works: **The Fall of the House of Usher, The Murders in the Rue Morgue, A Descent into the Maelström...** Poe and his wife lived in five different houses in Philadelphia, of which only one is still standing, in the **Northern Liberties** district. Drawings on the wall stand in for the long-gone furniture. Ardent Poe fans will want to visit the lower floor which shares strange similarities with the basement described in his short story The Black Cat. If The Raven is more your bag, you may choose to declaim verses in front of the statue of the black bird, its wings extended, erected outside the building: Nevermore.

Edgar Allan Poe National Historical Site – *532 N. 7th St. - ℘ (215) 965-2305 - www.nps.gov/edal/index.htm - Fri-Sun 9am-12pm, 1pm-5pm - admission free.*

world's oldest steel warship afloat and the sole surviving vessel of the Spanish-American War (1898), and the **USS Becuna**, a WWII submarine. Open to visitors since 2016, the **Diligence** is a 31-m-long schooner from the 18th century, reconstructed by volunteers and presented in an exhibition on the American Revolution and its pirate problem.

Hill-Physick House ★

G6 *321 S. 4th St. - ℘ (215) 925 7866 - www.philalandmarks.org - Apr-Nov: guided tour hourly, Thu-Sat 11am-3pm, Sun 12pm-3pm; rest of year: enquire - $8 (children $6).*
Purchased in 1815 by the "father of American surgery", Dr Philip Syng Physick, this four-story townhouse (1786) was home to the Physick family until 1940 when it was bequeathed to Pennsylvania Hospital. In the 1960s, well-known philanthropists Walter and Leonore Annenberg bought the property and transformed it into a model of the federal style. The exquisite period furniture illustrates the life of the upper echelons of society during Victorian times.

Pennsylvania Hospital – *800 Spruce St. - guided tour, enquire before visiting.* Dr. Physick worked and taught in this institution, a stone's throw from his residence, founded in 1751 by Benjamin Franklin and Dr. Thomas Bond. You can visit the amphitheater where he taught or simply admire the red brick exterior considered to be one of the nation's finest examples of the colonial style.

NORTH OF PENN'S LANDING

Fishtown

Fishtown is another of Philly's historic districts, located northeast of Center City. It was named in homage to its former life as a commercial fishing center for shad, one of the easiest and most productive fish to catch in these parts. While exploring the neighborhood, have fun seeing how many decorative wooden fish displaying house numbers you can spot. Symbolic of the industrial revolution and known for its social uprisings, the district has welcomed wave after wave of Irish, Polish, and German immigrants and was once inhabited by a large proportion of their descendants, then laborers, artisans, and middle-class employees. Completely overlooked during Philly's redevelopment in the late 20th century, Fishtown profited in the 2000s from the real estate and artistic boom of its neighbor, Northern Liberties. The district has been in regeneration ever since. The charming lanes lined with period houses contrast beautifully with the elevated subway line and modern residences. Gentrification has brought a new wave of young professionals, hipsters, and all sorts of creatives to a neighborhood that was already thriving and

Jon Bilous/Getty Images Plus

Ships in Penn's Landing.

cosmopolitan. Benches and swings in the public parks continue to attract cool families out walking and single folk practicing crossfit or participating in group yoga sessions. If you're on the hunt for vintage stores, trendy bars and restaurants, and organic or vegan places, there's no shortage of them along the main commercial streets and bustling side streets.

Northern Liberties

Northern Liberties connects Old City to Philly's northeastern districts. It extends from Girard Avenue to Callowhill Street north to south, and from the Delaware River to 6th Street east to west. Once a thriving industrial area of factories, warehouses, textiles manufacturers, tanneries, and breweries, it fell out of favor among post-war Philadelphians until the 1990s when it thrived once more, albeit artistically. A progressive band of avant-garde artists chose to migrate to the north of the city, lured by the fusion of industrial architecture and period charm, and more importantly the still affordable and unoccupied spaces where they could open studios and galleries. Developers and architects then followed, rushing to put up new spaces for living which showcased the very best of contemporary design blended with environmental credentials. Since then, the district hasn't looked back and the value of **NoLibs**, as it is known by the locals, has not stopped climbing and luring in entrepreneurs and creatives. Residents and travelers alike flock to the neighborhood's eateries, bars, and art and cultural venues. The dynamism of Northern Liberties has produced a snowfall effect on its easy-going neighbor, Fishtown, which, little by little, might even steal NoLibs' thunder.

Center City ★★ and Washington Square★

Bookended north and south by Vine Street and Pine Street respectively, Center City has been Philadelphia's main commercial district since the 1870s, when the current city hall was constructed. Multiple new developments went up about a century later with a view to revive the area. One of the oldest indoor markets in the U.S., Reading Terminal Market is the district's food epicenter. Nearby Chinatown has an abundance of tempting food options too. Further south and more residential, Midtown Village and Gayborhood are filled with lively places to eat or dance, and historic brick buildings festooned with rainbow flags. Elegant and tree-lined Washington Square marks the transition between the center and Independence National Historical Park, of which it is now part. Hands down one of the most charming areas in Philadelphia. By contrast, blue-collar South Philly abounds with multicultural diversity, no better represented than the bustling Italian Market.

▶**Getting there:** Ⓜ 15th (City Hall), 13th and 8th on the Market-Frankford Line. 5th Station for Washington Square. Trolley Line, 15th Station for City Hall.

Local Map p. 40. Detachable Map EFG4-5.

▶**Tip:** Reading Terminal Market makes the ideal starting point for your Center City exploration: its 80 food merchants and non-stop buzz is a must-experience for foodies that won't break the bank.

CENTER CITY★★

City Hall ★

E5 1400 John F. Kennedy Blvd, between 15th St. and 13th St. - ℰ (215) 686 2840 - www.phila.gov - to see interior pieces, guided tours run Mon-Fri at 12:30pm - admission free. Taking up a whole block in Center City, this French Second Empire-style structure is the largest municipal building in the U.S. With close to 700 rooms, it was designed by architect John McArthur Jr. At its completion in 1901, the gigantic masonry building was already considered unfashionable and there were plans to tear it down. The exorbitant demolition costs put paid to that proposal. City Hall remains the beloved "palace of honor" of Philadelphia. Its 548-foot tower is

WHERE TO EAT

Reading Terminal Market ... ❶
McGillin's Olde Ale House ... ❷
Dim Sum Garden .... ❸
Penang .... ❹
Talula's Garden .... ❺
Revolution Taco .... ❻
Prunella..................... ❼
Masala Kitchen .... ❽
Green Eggs Café............. ❾
K'far Cafe .... ❿
Grandma's Philly .... ⓫
Urban Farmer .... ⓬
XIX Nineteen .... ⓭
Veda .... ⓮
Vedge....................... ⓯
Vernick Fish .... ⓰
Oyster House................ ⓱
Her Place Supper Club ..... ⓲
The Love .... ⓳
Jean-Georges Philadelphia.. ⓴
White Dog Cafe............. ㊳
Friday Saturday Sunday..... ㊶
Di Bruno Bros............... ㊻

WHERE TO DRINK

High Street Philly .... ❶

Federal Donuts.............. ❷
Jeni's Splendid Ice Cream ... ❸
Mayflower
  Café & Bakery .... ❹
Leda and The Swan .... ⓫
Wet Deck Philly............. ⓮
JG SkyHigh.................. ⓯
El Techo .... ⓰
Independence
  Beer Garden................ ⓲

SHOPPING

Reading Terminal Market ... ❷
Rittenhouse Square
  Farmer's Market .... ❹
Macy's .... ❺
Fashion District
  Philadelphia................ ❻
P's and Q's.................. ❾
NewsBoy Hats............... ⓫
Antique Row .... ⓱

NIGHTLIFE

Kimmel Cultural Campus ... ❶
Walnut Street Theater....... ❷
South .... ❸

Velvet Whip .... ❹
Chris' Jazz Cafe .... ❺
Time .... ❻
Tabu Lounge and
  Sports Bar................. ❼
The Trestle Inn.............. ❽

WHERE TO STAY

Hyatt Centric Hotel .... ❶
The Guild House............. ❷
Sonder at The Arco .... ❸
The Notary Hotel
  Autograph Collection...... ❹
Loews Philadelphia Hotel ... ❺
Four Seasons Hotel Philadelphia
  at Comcast Center......... ❻
W Philadelphia .... ❼
Sonesta Rittenhouse
  Square .... ❽
Element Philadelphia
  Downtown................. ❾
Cornerstone B&B .... ⓫
The Study at
  University City............. ⓬

41

topped by a huge statue of William Penn, the founder of Philadelphia. A single lock of hair is almost 16 inches long! Noteworthy features of the building include: **Mayor's Reception Room** with its mahogany wainscoting and **Conversation Hall** whose ceiling is decorated with aluminum leaves.

Masonic Temple ★

E4 *1 N. Broad St., north of City Hall - ℘ (215) 988 1900 - pamasonictemple. org - guided tours Tue-Sat at 10am, 11am, 1pm, 2pm and 3pm - $15 (-12s $5).* Regarded as one of the most beautiful Masonic temples in the U.S.—it's also one of the world's largest–, this granite building in the medieval Norman style, featuring spires and towers, was designed by Brother James Windrim. The incredibly diverse interior decor was inspired by the emblems of the Masonic lodges. The second-floor museum has a fascinating collection of documents and artefacts, including one of two of Brother George Washington's Masonic aprons. This item loaded with symbols (red signifying courage, blood, life; blue eternity, loyalty, immortality; white purity and innocence; the eye his Divine watchfulness; the beehive industriousness, etc.) is a symbol itself in the Masonic world: based on a stonemason's apron, it reminds Freemasons to never be idle and always lead an active life.

Reading Terminal Market★

F4 *N. 12th St. and Arch St. - readingterminalmarket.org - 8am-6pm.*

Completed in 1893, this indoor market was long the main site for Philadelphians to do their grocery shopping, home to as many as 350 merchants, before falling into decline in the 1970s. It was restored to its former glory, structurally and commercially, in 1993, when the **Pennsylvania Convention Center** *(1101 Arch St.)* was built and the historic market premises were preserved. The Amish community sell produce (except on Sunday) from their farms. Stock up on excellent cheese, jams, and other homemade goodies. It's also a destination for a typical American breakfast of pancakes and other classics at **Down Home Diner**, lunch–options include an oyster bar, barbecue sandwich vendor, or vegan stand–, or locally produced food souvenirs to take home.

CHINATOWN

F4 *The district extends northeast from the Convention Center.*

Established in 1860, it's the second-largest Chinatown on the East Coast. It has a population of 3,000, predominantly descendants of migrants from China, Taiwan, Vietnam, South Korea, Myanmar, and Malaysia. **Friendship Gate** may look old with its traditional Chinese dragons and ideograms, but it was actually built in 1984. It was a gift from Tianjin, a city twinned with Philadelphia, and makes a colorful portal to the neighborhood *(corner of Arch St. and N 10th St.)*. Most people gravitate to Chinatown for its countless Pan-Asian restaurants, but it's also popular for its beauty salons, Korean treatments especially.

It's a festive place too, hosting the **Chinese Lantern Festival** on **Franklin Square** and Chinese New Year.

African American Museum in Philadelphia

F4 *701 Arch St. - ℘ (215) 574 0380 - www.aampmuseum.org - Thu-Sun 10am-5pm - $14 (ages 4-12, students and seniors $10).*

This museum was the first municipal institution funded to preserve and exhibit the heritage of African Americans. It shares this community's history, including their arrival in Philadelphia, through the lens of major developments in American society: the civil rights movement, arts and entertainments, sport, medicine, architecture, politics, religion, and so forth. A counter-history that puts a spotlight on figures unfairly overlooked by official history, like **Edmonia Lewis** (1844-1907), the first female African American and Native American sculptor to achieve international prominence with her neoclassical-style sculpture. Or **Julian Abele** (1881-1950), an eminent African American architect who designed many a monumental building including Philadelphia's **Free Library**. The museum presents a complex and often contradictory history with masterly nuance, even with regard to some of its most illustrious figures. George Washington, for instance, who supported the gradual abolition of slavery, was himself a major landholder and owned over 300 slaves. He freed all his enslaved people in his will when he died.

WASHINGTON SQUARE ★

F5 One of the most beautiful and pleasant neighborhoods in Philadelphia... not to mention one of the oldest. It was part of the original city plan devised by William Penn for Philadelphia. The park sits on the site of an old cemetery where victims of the American Revolution were buried. The **Tomb of the Unknown Soldier** is a war memorial in their honor. A perfect spot for a breather or picnic.

It's a delight to take a stroll along the charming streets around the square, lined with trees bearing dazzling leaves in fall. With an abundance of shops, these streets are a window-shopping paradise, especially **Antique Row** (*Pine St., between S. 9th St. and S. 12th St.*), whose name is less representative of the stores that trade there today.

MIDTOWN VILLAGE AND GAYBORHOOD

The aptly named **Midtown Village** lies roughly between Rittenhouse Square and Washington Square.

As you venture in, you'll spot numerous buildings draped with rainbow flags, a sure sign you have entered Midtown's LGBTQ+ district: **Gayborhood**. This is the epicenter of Philadelphia's LGBTQ+ community, packed with shops, clubs, bars, and restaurants, and the site of the oldest theater in the United States:
Walnut Street Theatre
(*⊙ Addresses p. 98*).

SOUTH STREET AND SOUTH PHILLY

South Street

DG6 The southern border of Society Hill, this colorful street has led the city's counter-culture since the 1960s. The blocks between the Delaware River and 10th Street offer a string of places to shop, eat, or dance.

Philadelphia's Magic Gardens ★

F6 *1020 South St. - ℘ (215) 733 0390 - phillymagicgardens.org - Wed-Mon 11am-6pm - $15*
(ages 6-12 $8) - play areas for children.
Created by Philadelphian artist **Isaiah Zagar** (1939-), famed for his mosaics, this labyrinth-like garden decorated with pieces of glass, mirrors, and porcelain will enchant you as you spy mermaids, animals, and poetic messages along your tour.
The neighboring streets also feature mosaics, which you can locate using the map provided at the entrance.

Open-Air Painting

Starting out in 1984, the **Mural Arts Philadelphia** program has covered the city in over **4,000 murals,** making it the biggest open-air museum worldwide.

GRAFFITI BE GONE!

It's 1984. The city in crisis is easy prey for graffiti. A worsening blight on the urban landscape, it indiscriminately strikes prestigious monuments and abandoned buildings. The municipality responded by inviting **Jane Golden** (*G p. 16*) to run a program to find alternative ways for graffiti writers to contribute to the city. The aim was to channel their creative energy so they could self-express while transforming the public space. The idea—to which graffiti artists were initially skeptical—was a success and has since been integrated into social welfare programs. In collaboration with the municipality, community centers, schools, churches, and religious congregations, Mural Arts Philadelphia is involved with deprived neighborhoods and homeless shelters, and even has a training program in prisons. They train those at society's fringes to paint or lay bricks, helping them acquire a trade and find employment.

ORGANIZED WALLS

Philadelphia's murals are not only the work of vulnerable citizens. Many were created by known artists, invited and not always paid but always supported by funds donated by the public. These artworks are fragile: not only are they exposed to the elements, they are frequently painted on walls of private buildings. So they could disappear with the next construction or demolition. This only seems to add to their unique and appealing quality.

HOW TO SEE THEM

The murals are dotted all across the city, some in districts that are more remote or less-frequented and aspiring to gentrification now the artists have moved in. If you're downtown, explore one of two **Mural Mile** routes between City Center, Chinatown, Midtown Village, and Old City, where you can see 30 or so murals (*download a map online from www.muralarts.org/self-guided - takes around an hour*). One of the most iconic is **Philadelphia Muses** by Meg Saligman (*1999 - 1235 Locust St.*), filled with figures who have contributed to the city's history. The more recent **Untitled** (*2019 - 1108 Sansom St.*) by artist Amy Sherald, best known for painting the official portrait of Michelle Obama exhibited at the National Portrait Gallery, is impressive to say the least. Six-stories tall, the mural depicts an African American North Philly student symbolizing the elegance and determination of the future generation of African American women.
Info: www.muralarts.org. G Addresses, Visits (G p. 116).

44

Flight by Tatyana Fazlalizadeh at 1228 Spruce Street.

The Mummers Parade

Every January 1, thousands of Philadelphians in colorful costumes strut along Broad Street to celebrate the new year. Over 40 Mummers Clubs participate in the Parade, divided into five divisions: The Comic, The Fancy, the Fancy Brigade, the String Band, and the Wench Brigade Divisions. Over 10,000 people dedicate tons of time and effort through the year to plan the elaborate costumes, accessories, and moveable scenery, as each year has a new theme.

The tradition is said to have its roots in the first Swedish immigrants who arrived in the late 17th century. A vital part of Philadelphian life for over 200 years, the official Mummers Parade was ordained by the city in 1901. The Mummers Parade has moved with the times, now embracing previously underrepresented communities. Several Latino, African American, drag queen, and LGBTQ+ clubs have taken part in recent parades.

The Mummers Parade begins at City Hall before heading south along Broad Street through to Washington Avenue.

South Philly and Italian Market

46

F7 *9th St., between Christian St. and Wharton St. - no. 47 bus from Washington Square - italianmarketphilly.org.*

This district of Philadelphia has always been a magnet for immigrants, first the Irish, then the Italian. Philadelphia still has a big Italian community who have made a profound mark on South Philly's culture. The essence of this impact is distilled in the **Italian Market**. Foodies come to stock up from a vast array of fresh products, many of which are sourced from Italy. You also eat well here, whether for a quick snack or more elaborate meal. Or delve deeper into the foodie scene on a tour led by the vivacious Jacqueline. An Italian native from these parts, trained chef Jacquie (to her friends) knows every stand and street, and will take you on a tour to taste cheese, cold cuts, pizza, cannoli, and even tacos. Because the district's identity has followed migration patterns, today Italian coffee roasters happily rub shoulders with Mexican restaurants and Asian merchants. A multicultural dimension that fits well with Philadelphia and its spirit of tolerance and cosmopolitan vibes.

Jacqueline Kelly, food tour – *www.streatsofphillyfoodtours.com.*

K. Huff/PHLCVB

Italian Market, South Philadelphia.

Mummers Museum

G7 *1100 S. 2ⁿᵈ St./Washington Ave - bus no. 57 (3ʳᵈ & Market St.) - ℘ (215) 336 3050 - www.mummersmuseum.com - Tue-Fri 10am-5pm, Sat 10am-3pm.* Inside are elaborate costumes worn during the annual Mummers Parade on New Year's Day, a colorful tradition brought over by Scandinavian immigrants in the 17th century. Museum visitors can learn about the five divisions of Mummers *(see box)* and their unusual customs, such as the correct way to walk or "strut" and the significance of "Golden Slippers".

Benjamin Franklin Parkway ★★★ and Rittenhouse Square★

Designed to emulate the Champs-Élysées in Paris, the boulevard runs from City Hall to the Philadelphia Museum of Art. The great many museums along this stretch of roadway have earned it the moniker **Museum Row**. Leafy, very wide, and embellished by numerous monuments and sculptures, it's a boulevard made for strolling, quietly contemplating the beauty of the place or going for a run if you're feeling athletic. Between Benjamin Franklin Parkway and Rittenhouse Square, west of City Hall, Philly is graced with a skyline to rival that of any great American metropolis with its soaring skyscrapers, banks, and business towers. Yet old patrician Philadelphia with its brick houses is never far away, and Rittenhouse Square, one of the city's most stunning parks, is a chic haven of peace, mostly residential and home to some of the city's finest restaurants.

48

▶**Getting there:** Benjamin Franklin Parkway is poorly served by the subway. Ⓜ 15th at City Hall is the closest station to Logan Circle. More convenient are the PHLASH and SEPTA bus services 32, 38, and 48. The number 38 bus travels along the entire parkway.

Detachable Map CDEF3-5.

▶**Tip:** To appreciate the full view of the Benjamin Franklin Parkway, go to the top of the steps at the Philadelphia Museum of Art, with the City Hall bell tower in your line of sight. Else head to JFK Plaza and stand in front of the LOVE Sculpture (Ⓖ see box). Set aside two whole days to explore the city's main museums.

BENJAMIN FRANKLIN PARKWAY★★★

DEF3-4 Peppered with commemorative monuments including the statue of Polish patriot **Tadeusz Kościuszko** (1977) and the **Civil War Soldiers and Sailors Monument** (1927), the Benjamin Franklin Parkway traverses **Logan Circle** (in the far southeast), where stands the **Swann Memorial Fountain** by American sculptor Alexander Calder, and the **Free Library of Philadelphia** (1927) by Horace Trumbauer, one of two buildings (at the corner of 19th St. and Vine St.) modeled on structures on Place de la Concorde in Paris. The avenue is adorned by 109 flags of countries around the world representing the immigrant communities that call Philadelphia home. They are arranged alphabetically, with the exception of five—for example, Israel's flag hangs in front of the Holocaust Memorial. France's is outside the Rodin Museum (*G* p.52).

Pennsylvania Academy of the Fine Arts ★★

E4 *118-218 N. Broad St. - ✆ (215) 972 7600 - www.pafa.org - Thu-Fri 10am-4pm, Sat-Sun 11am-5pm - $18 (ages 13-18 $10, -12s free).*
The nation's oldest art museum and art school, the Academy was founded in 1805 by the painter Charles Willson Peale (1741-1827) and the sculptor William Rush (1756-1833), modeled on the Fine Arts Academy in London. The collections and temporary exhibitions which cover in chronological order over three centuries of American art are spread over two separate buildings.
The **main building** *(entrance)* is a brick-and-limestone structure (1876, Frank Furness and George Hewitt), remarkable in every respect. There you'll find artworks from the 18th to the first half of the 20th century. As you peruse the exhibits, which change several times a year, you can admire works by **Mary Cassatt**, much inspired by the French Impressionists, **John Singer Sargent**, a prominent portrait artist, **Winslow Homer**, best known for his marine subjects, and many others less known outside the U.S. Some

The LOVE Sculpture

No trip to Philadelphia is complete without a selfie or photo in front of Robert Indiana's iconic sculpture. Installed in 1976 on **JFK Plaza**, this sculpture has been reproduced in many major metropolises, including New York, Madrid, Montreal, and Singapore to name a few.
It also conveniently marks the start of the Benjamin Franklin Parkway and affords the best perspective.

pieces, due to their size and scale, are permanently on show, like *Penn's Treaty with the Indians*★ by **Benjamin West** (1772), which depicts the legendary meeting between William Penn and the Lenape, or the life-size portrait of George Washington painted by **Gilbert Stuart**, also named the *Lansdowne Portrait*★★ (1796).
The neighboring **Samuel M. V. Hamilton Building** (2006), with large picture windows and vast exhibition spaces, is almost entirely devoted to art from the 1950s and sculpture. The first floor is given over to temporary exhibitions, the second, following the same principle of regularly flipped exhibits, features works by artists such as **Richard Diebenkorn** and **Roy Lichtenstein**.

Cathedral Basilica of Saints Peter and Paul ★

E4 *1723 Race St. (N. 18th St.).*
The mother church of the Archdiocese of Philadelphia is a Renaissance-style cathedral from 1864 modeled after

49

San Carlo al Corso Church in Rome. Inside are a magnificent coffered barrel-vaulted ceiling forming an arch over the transept and nave and an oculus painted by Constantino Brumidi. Its copper dome raised 155 ft from the ground has a beautifully decorative mural of The Assumption of the Virgin into Heaven.

The Comcast Center Campus

E4 1800 Arch St. - comcastcentercampus.com.
This newly opened campus consists of five buildings, although the Comcast Center (corner of 17th St. and John F. Kennedy Blvd) and the Comcast Technology Center are the main attraction. With 58 and 60 stories respectively, they are the city's tallest towers. Designed by Steven Spielberg and DreamWorks Animation among others (free same day-only reservation), **The Universal Sphere**, located inside the Comcast Technology Center, is a 360-degree immersive experience featuring a short film about the power of ideas through the history of various well-known celebrities. Internationally renowned artists the likes of Jenny Holzer and Conrad Shawcross have created artworks for the Comcast Technology Center. The skyscraper also contains several restaurants and a luxury hotel (ⓒ p. 82 and 102). The **Comcast Experience** is installed in the Comcast Center lobby. This jumbo, state-of-the-art, 27-million pixel display is one of the world's largest LED continuous video walls.

Visitors can enjoy a variety of free programming all year round.

Academy of Natural Sciences of Drexel University ★

E4 1900 Benjamin Franklin Pkwy, on Logan Circle - ℘ (215) 299 1000 - www.ansp.org - Wed-Fri 10am-4:30pm, Sat-Sun 10am-5pm - $27 (ages 2-12 $23) - visit website for discounted tickets.
This natural history museum is at the leading edge of scientific research and houses one of the world's biggest collections: over 18 million specimens, including 10 million shells and mollusks, 4 million insects, 1 million fossils, not to mention specimens collected by Meriwether Lewis and William Clark during their coast-to-coast American expedition (1804-1806), and the first dinosaur skeleton unearthed in the U.S.—a treasure of which only a few bones were actually discovered. The museum offers plenty to do and visitors can partake in all kinds of activities through the year.
On the first floor, the **Dinosaur Hall**★ is one of the most fascinating areas where visitors can view all kinds of skeletons and fossils, plus see how paleontologists dig up bones and study them in the lab. Head to the **Fossil Prep Lab** for permission to touch ancient specimens, or to the Time Machine to have a photo with dinosaurs scrolling behind you. A selection of life-size **dioramas** provide a window into the natural habitat of native species of North

America (*1st floor*), Asia and Africa (*2nd floor*). Up on level 3, **Outside In** is ideal for younger visitors, letting them get up close and even touch different animals (never the same ones) from rabbits to turtles to snakes.

The Franklin Institute ★

D4 *222 North 20th St. - ☎ (215) 448 1200 - www.fi.edu - 9:30am-5pm - various ticket options, from $23.*
The Franklin Institute, founded in 1824 to teach science to artisans and mechanics, really knows how to make science fun. Visitors enter the museum via the **Benjamin Franklin National Memorial**, a rotunda dominated by a dramatic 20-foot marble statue of Philadelphia's much admired Founding Father.
The three exhibition floors cover subjects as varied as **communications**, transport, **computer science**, **space**, **natural phenomena**, **geology**, and the **human body**. Don't leave before you touch a real meteorite which fell to Earth in Arizona 50 million years ago and is estimated to be over 5 billion years old—500 million years older than the Sun. The oldest known object on the planet! The two-story-tall Giant Heart is another captivating exhibit. The complex includes a **planetarium** and two **IMAX cinema theaters** in addition to a program of temporary exhibitions and experiences such as the **Escape Rooms** in which visitors are "locked in" and have to use their ingenuity to solve various puzzles and tasks to be let out. A whole world of fun. You won't be alone, far from it,

and, if you're traveling with kids, you can bet your bottom dollar that a visit will be one of the vacation highlights with so much to see, do and, for a change, touch! The museum shop is an Aladdin's cave of tempting gift ideas.

Barnes Foundation ★★★

D4 *2025 Benjamin Franklin Pkwy - ☎ (215) 278 7000 - www.barnesfoundation.org - Thu-Mon 11am-5pm - $30 (ages 13-18 $5, seniors $28) - download the app on your smartphone.*
☺ The Foundation ticket office offers a restricted number of tickets daily. For guaranteed admission, book on site or in advance online.
Up until 2012, you had to travel to Merion, in the Philadelphia suburbs, to admire the Barnes Foundation's collection, the largest body of **Impressionist and post-Impressionist paintings★★★** ever assembled by a private collector. An extraordinary man in multiple respects, **Albert C. Barnes** (1872-1951), born penniless in Philadelphia, became a doctor before inventing a revolutionary antiseptic that earned him his fortunes. Dr. Barnes was an art enthusiast, a shrewd collector, an art theorist, and an educator, believing that every person was entitled to an education and knowledge of the fine arts. To this end, he set up in 1922 a foundation in his name, then a museum which was intended to show his collection to a select audience–factory workers, the uneducated, and African Americans.

After his accidental death, Barnes' Merion mansion was opened to the wider public, with limited daily admissions given the small size of the building.

In 2012, the collection was moved to a **new edifice**—a stunning contemporary geometric building designed by the architects Tod Williams and Billie Tsien–but, as dictated by the conditions of Barnes' will, the artworks had to be displayed exactly as they had been: the paintings are arranged in precisely the same way, even down to their orientation and the size of the gap between works. It's a successful museum, managing to remain personal, almost intimate, despite its dimensions. Barnes prioritized the juxtaposition of shapes and colors rather than grouping works by artist. Interestingly, there are no labels for the paintings, a decision made so visitors can enjoy the works with an open mind and according to their own tastes. As such, we recommend you download the museum app on your smartphone via the QR code at the entrance or on the website *barnesfoc. us*. Use your phone's camera to identify a painting that catches your eye and information about the piece will be instantly displayed on your screen. Visitors are free to explore the museum galleries in any order they like, without the rigid circuit typical of traditional museums. Enter your email address and all of the artworks you viewed via the app will be sent to your inbox with their commentary, making a wonderful

souvenir. The app also lets you share pieces you are interested in with your friends during your visit.

As you explore the 20 rooms set over two floors, you can view **181 Renoirs**, **69 Cézannes**, **59 Matisses**, **46 Picassos**, **21 Soutines**, **18 Rousseaus**, **16 Modiglianis**, among the most represented artists, along with paintings by Rubens, Goya, Manet, Van Gogh, and De Chirico, to name but a few, African objects (statuettes, textiles, etc.), Egyptian, Greek, and Roman antiquities, and furniture and decorative pieces that adorned Barnes' mansion.

The Artist's Family (1896) and *Jeanne Durand-Ruel* (1876) by **Renoir**, *The Card Players* (1892) by **Cézanne**, *The Joy of Life* (1906), and *Studio with Goldfish* (1912) by **Matisse**, *The Ascetic* (1903) by Picasso, *The Models* (1888) by **Seurat**, *The Postman* (1889) by **Van Gogh,** and *Reclining Nude from the Back* (1917) by **Modigliani**, are undoubtedly the best known works in the collection, but there's not enough room to mention them all. Following their nose (or eyes rather), each visitor gets to appreciate the masterpieces in keeping with their interests and current mood, as Barnes intended.

Rodin Museum ★

D3-4 *2151 Benjamin Franklin Pkwy (between N. 21ˢᵗ and N. 22ⁿᵈ St.) - ☏ (215) 763 8100 - www. rodinmuseum.org - Fri-Mon 10am-5pm - the entry fee is voluntary, although the suggested donation is $12.*

🙂 A free shuttle *(corner of N. 22nd St.)* connects the Rodin Museum and the Philadelphia Museum of Art hourly. Or if you prefer to walk, you can amble from one to the other in under 15 minutes. The museum does not have a cafeteria.

Set in a stunning Beaux Arts-style building from the 1920s designed by the architect Paul Cret, this museum houses the largest collection of artworks by **Auguste Rodin** (1840-1917) outside France. It was the brainchild of art collector, entrepreneur and philanthropist Jules E. Mastbaum, an enthusiastic admirer of the French sculptor. In the exquisite **garden**, a peaceful oasis designed by French architect and landscaper Jacques Gréber, and four galleries, visitors can see over a hundred pieces, beautifully showcased and covering every period of the work of the man described as the father of modern sculpture. One room is dedicated to **Balzac**, an author Rodin was fascinated by and whose commemorative statue was poorly received at its unveiling (1898). Don't miss the famous **Gates of Hell**, the iconic **Thinker**, inspired by Dante's *The Divine Comedy*, and **The Kiss**.

Philadelphia Museum of Art
★★★

D3 *2600 Benjamin Franklin Pkwy (corner of N. 26th St.)* - 📞 *(215) 763 8100 - philamuseum.org - Thu and Sat-Mon 10am-5pm, Fri 10am-8:45pm - $25 (-18s free) - shuttle to the Rodin Museum once an hour.*

At the north end of the Benjamin Franklin Parkway, this majestic Greek Revival building (1928) houses one of the richest art museums in the U.S., built in 1876 for the Centennial International Exhibition. It now has over 225,000 objects (not all on display), divided between four main departments: Asian Art, American Art, European Art, and Modern & Contemporary Art.

The reorganization of the museum, designed by **Frank Gehry**, was completed in 2021: brand new spaces and galleries have been added, centered around a spectacular hall and sculptural switchback staircase.

American Art and Modern & Contemporary Art are set over the 1st and 2nd floors – American art has been at the heart of the collection since the institution was founded in 1876. The evolution of furniture design and art from the European colonial period to the genesis of typically American art is one of the most fascinating sections. From portraits by Copley, one of the first American painters, to ceramics by Rookwood, produced since 1880 in Cincinnati, Ohio, the rooms devoted to **American art★★★** offer an incredibly rich trove of artworks. Notable exhibits include often locally produced furniture and silverware, like the Shaker pieces (late 18th which furnished the interiors of rigorist settlers who shook before God). Portraitist **Charles Willson Peale** is well represented, as is **Thomas Eakins**, author of **The Gross

Clinic★★ (1876). Another compelling piece is **The Annunciation★** by **Henry Ossawa Tanner** (1898) depicting Mary as a young Middle Eastern woman. The artist, trained by Eakins, was the first African American student to attend the Pennsylvania Academy of the Fine Arts, but he moved to France due to the limited opportunities open to him in his county of birth.

European Art 1850-1900 (Impressionism) on the 2nd floor – Carpeaux, Corot, the Barbizon School, Degas, Monet, Seurat, Morisot, Vuillard, Bonnard, Braque, Delaunay, Léger... French artists dominate the **European Art** department ★★ and are equally abundant in the modern and contemporary art galleries. Notable mentions include **The Bathers★★★** by **Cézanne** (1894 1905), a masterly reinterpretation of the genre that creates a link between classical art and modern painting; **Sunflowers★★** by **Van Gogh** (1890); **Three Musicians★★★** by **Picasso** (1921) and countless works by **Marcel Duchamp**, of which some, like **The Large Glass★★★** (1915 1923), were installed by the artist in person.

European Art (Medieval to Romanticism) - Asian Art – Arms and Armor on the 3rd floor – The rooms devoted to European Art through the Renaissance present a remarkable collection of architectural features from monasteries (Saint-Genix de Fontanes, Saint-Michel de Cuxa) and chapels (stained glass from Sainte-Chapelle), along with religious paintings and sculptures, including a **diptych★★** by **Van der Weyden** (c. 1460) and **Saint Francis of Assisi Receiving the Stigmata★** by **Van Eyck** (c. 1430). The galleries for the following period hold several reproductions of Flemish, English, French, and Italian interiors alongside a superb selection of artworks, from Pinturicchio to Titian by way of Rubens, Poussin, Vouet, and Chardin, and an astonishing Head of Christ painted by

54

A Selfie with Rocky Balboa?

An unexpected host welcomes visitors at the bottom of the 72-step staircase leading up to the **Philadelphia Museum of Art**: the **statue of Rocky Balboa** (1980), the fictional boxer made flesh by **Sylvester Stallone** in the famous film franchise (1976-2006). Perhaps not as unexpected as all that for anyone who has seen the first movie and remembers the iconic scene where Rocky runs to the top of the steps at dawn after a punishing training session. The athlete turns to face Philly, fists in the air, ready to conquer the world. The steps, a symbol of perseverance, has become a legendary site since Stallone donated the statue to the city. After many discussions and despite pushback from conservators, the foot of the steps was the chosen spot! Don't feel obliged to run up the stairs yourself. Crowds rush to the Rocky statue where a selfie or photo in front of the sculpture has become a rite of passage for lots of tourists from all over, who only know Philadelphia through the films.

K. Huff/PHLCVB

Statue of Rocky Balboa, by A. Thomas Schomberg.

Rembrandt (c. 1656), discovered in the museum's reserves just several years ago.

In the Asian Art galleries, highlights include a reconstruction of a **17th-century Palace Reception Hall**★★ from Beijing, with its stunning painted paneling; and the exceptional **Sunkaraku ceremonial teahouse**★★★ (v. 1917), brought over from Tokyo.

RITTENHOUSE SQUARE ★

E5 Rittenhouse Square is one of the five squares **William Penn** included in his city plan in the late 17th century. Without question the most prestigious, it lends the neighborhood its elegant and well-to-do atmosphere. Come here to escape the bustling city. With its magnificent trees and welcoming benches, it's a perfect spot for an al fresco lunch, which you can cobble together on the fly by ordering takeout from the many restaurants surrounding the picturesque park. The square has a number of statues including Lion Crushing a Serpent by the French sculptor **Antoine-Louis Barye**.

Rittenhouse Square holds a **farmers market** bursting with fresh, local produce (Sat and Wed 10am-2pm). It's also an upscale shopping destination with Tiffany & Co., Rag & Bone, Anthropologie, and other high-end brands in the vicinity.

One Liberty Place

E5 *1650 Market Pl.* Recognizable by its silver spire evoking the Chrysler Building in New York, this skyscraper was the first building taller than the Penn Statue atop City Hall. Its construction from 1984 to 1987 symbolized the city's new regeneration.

South Broad Street is home to many a concert venue, including the **Academy of Music** (1857) *(240 S Broad St. - ℘ (215) 893 1999 - www. academyofmusic.org).*

Mütter Museum and Garden ★

D5 *19 S. 22nd St. - ℘ (215) 563.3737 - muttermuseum.org - 10am-5pm - $20.* Doctor and innovative surgeon **Thomas Dent Mütter** (1811-1859) was also a passionate collector. He accumulated through his life all sorts of specimens, casts, skeletons, and publications in the field of medicine, totaling 1,700 pieces that he left in his will to the College of Physicians, the city's medical academy, with the intention of starting a museum. Inaugurated in 1863 and subsequently installed in this building, the museum is the largest of its kind nationally.

Originally intended to share scientific knowledge, the museum is also a cabinet of curiosities that is sure to please younger visitors with a penchant for the macabre things in life. If you're faint of heart, perhaps swerve some of the more grisly anatomical exhibits.

Highlights include a cast of the torso of the original "Siamese" twins who rose to fame in the 19th century, Chang and Eng, who married sisters and fathered 22 children between them. *The Soap Lady* is the naturally mummified body of a woman exhumed in 1875. In addition to a staggering collection of 139 skulls, the museum has on permanent display small segments of Albert Einstein's brain which, startlingly, weighed less than an average adult's.

The adjoining **Dr. Benjamin Rush Medicinal Plant Garden** contains more than 50 species.

NORTH END OF BENJAMIN FRANKLIN PARKWAY

Eastern State Penitentiary ★★

D2-3 *2027 Fairmount Ave - SEPTA bus no. 48, 43, 33, 32, 7, PHLASH bus or Big Bus - ℘ (215) 236 3300 - www. easternstate.org - 10am-5pm $17 (ages 7-12 $13) - book online in advance for discounted tickets.*

☺ Guided ghost-hunting tours are organized at night. For the ultimate immersive experience, we highly recommend coming for Halloween Nights (☾ *Festivals and Events p. 119*). There are so many reasons to visit this prison. This architectural monument from the 19th century, miraculously preserved, is as much a symbol of **successful heritage protection** as a captivating testament to the history of **incarceration theory**.

A Dog's Life

In 1924, a dog called Pep was jailed for life and even given a prison number: C-2559. Its crime? Allegedly killing the governor's wife's cat. That's the popular story. The true story is that Pep was gifted to the Eastern State Penitentiary as a therapy dog to improve the mental wellbeing of inmates. An explanation much more in tune with the penitentiary's progressive philosophy.

It all began in 1787 when Dr. Benjamin Rush, an expert on prisons, founded a prison reform group. Philadelphia already had a penitentiary on Chestnut Street where the conditions were particularly deplorable. Prisoners coexisted behind bars with no distinction made between age or gender. In 1821, the municipality approved the construction of a new jail, almost 2 miles from the city center: Eastern State Penitentiary, which welcomed its first prisoners eight years later.

The **prison model** akin to a medieval fortress was designed by the architect John Haviland, with cell blocks radiating from a central rotunda. It could hold 250 prisoners, who each had a cell and an individual yard. Their isolation was not designed to be punitive but to encourage them to "**do penance**" and reflect on their crime. Prisoners were made to wear a sack over their head so they wouldn't be recognized, making it then easier for them to rejoin society. Sentences were never very lengthy, several years at most. The **Pennsylvania model** was hailed as a success and over 300 prisons were soon built based on it in the U.S. and Europe. However, the heavily criticized solitary system was abandoned in 1913. Due to the growing prison population, cells and even entire floors were added to some buildings and it became standard practice for several prisoners to share a cell. Women were incarcerated in a separate prison from men from 1923, and the dilapidated penitentiary, where rioting and attempted escapes were not uncommon, was forced to close in 1971.

Since the site was partially reopened to the public in 1991, visitors can view the yards, corridors, hospital, places of worship catering to different faiths, and a few cells restored to their original state, including the relatively luxurious cell of **Al Capone**, who spent eight months behind bars there in 1929. Photos show the prison through the years. It's a unique experience that prompts you to think about the relationship between the prison system and criminality.

WEST OF RITTENHOUSE SQUARE

University City

BC5 *Leave Center City and cross over to the opposite bank of the Schuylkill River.* Ⓜ *The blue Market-Frankford Line, which stops at 30th St. and 34th St. The green Trolley Line also goes to 30th St. and 33rd St.*

This prestigious student area is home to the higher education institutions **Drexel University** and the world-famous **University of Pennsylvania**. The latter is a member of the famed **Ivy League**, a select circle of the eight most elite colleges in the U.S. Cream-of-the-crop students from around the country and indeed the world gravitate here all year round to live and study in a dynamic and vibrant atmosphere. Its leafy streets are lined with pretty Victorian houses, some now converted into bed and breakfasts (**☾** *Where to Stay, p. 103*). The public gardens are often filled with local residents practicing yoga, walking their dog, or reading on benches.

😊 The area truly comes to life at lunchtime. From food trucks sending out mouth-watering aromas to a host of fast-food restaurants to café bars set up in chic brownstones: choose your spot. Mingle with students, visiting parents, or professors marking assignments, and sit back and observe. After all, people-watching is as much a pastime here as American football! Lively conversations offer an authentic and immediate opportunity to immerse yourself into University City life.

Penn Museum

C6 *3260 South St. - ☎ (215) 898 4000 - www.penn.museum - Tue-Sun 10am-5pm - $18 (ages 6-17 $13).*
Penn Museum is an archaeology and anthropology museum and part of the University of Pennsylvania. Founded in 1887, the museum has always been at the center of anthropological research and continues to fund archaeological digs around the world. Many visitors might miss out if they don't take the trip out to University City, but we suggest you make the effort as it's one of the most revered and best documented museums devoted to the history of civilizations in the world. Inside over a million objects are exhibited or archived, including artefacts, books, parchments, sculptures, statues, and bronzes from the five continents. The evolution of civilizations is presented to visitors over two floors: Ancient Egypt, Greece and Rome, Mesopotamia, and Asia. In late 2019, the museum extended its collection, unveiling two additional galleries filled with exhibits on African, Pre-Colombian, and Native American civilizations. On the second floor is the not-to-be-missed gallery where you can view statues of Pharaohs, Buddhist sculptures, and Sumerian steles, some of which are inscribed with the earliest known writing in the history of humanity. Spectacular!

58

Philadelphia Museum of Art

Fairmount Park ★

Bordering the Philadelphia Museum of Art and extending from the Benjamin Franklin Parkway, Fairmount Park (1855) is a vast municipal park spread over more than 2,000 acres. Much of its charm comes from the Schuylkill River that runs through it. In 1876, it hosted the Centennial Exposition, the first World's Fair held in the U.S. It boasts the nation's oldest zoo, an arboretum (just one feature of the city's Horticulture Center there), Memorial Hall, and dozens of statues. It's a delightful refuge within easy reach of the bustling city where Philadelphians flock all year round to do all kinds of activities.

▶**Getting there:** SEPTA bus no. 7, 32, 33, 48 or PHLASH bus. Trolley no. 15 to get to the zoo.

Detachable Map BCD1-3.

▶**Tip:** Cycling is by far the best way to appreciate everything the park has to offer. It's a gorgeous site and a bike ride will take you to some of the most stunning views of Philadelphia (ⓖ *Philly by Bike p. 14*).

Fairmount Park hugs the Schuylkill River as it flows northeast and encompasses **Memorial Hall** *(corner of 42ⁿᵈ St. and N. Concourse Dr.)* – a Beaux-Arts-style building erected for the occasion of the Centennial Exposition of 1876 –, the **Azalea Garden** *(on Kelly Dr.)*, splendid in springtime, and the **Horticulture Center** *(corner of N. Horticultural and Montgomery Dr.)* featuring a traditional-style Japanese house, **Pine Breeze Villa★**.

The Fairmount Water Works and Boathouse Row ★

The Fairmount Water Works – As its name suggests, this was the hydraulic system used to supply water to the City of Philadelphia. Constructed between 1812 and 1815 on the east bank of the Schuylkill River, this industrial facility was encased in a neoclassical building, reflecting the tastes of the time. **Charles Dickens** referred to it as a "wondrous place" when he visited Philadelphia. The site affords clear views of **Boathouse Row★** *(Kelly Dr., along the Schuylkill, north of Azalea Garden - ℘ (215) 685 3936 - boathouserow.org)*. A row of a dozen boathouses and 19th-century houses, beautifully lit at night, house the city's rowing clubs. There's something quintessentially British about the place where watching the rowers glide along the Schuylkill River is a delight to behold.

Philadelphia Zoo ★

B2-3 *3400 W. Girard Ave - SEPTA bus no. 38, trolley no.15, PHLASH bus, or Big Bus - ℰ (215) 243 100 - www.philadelphiazoo.org - Mar-Oct: 9:30am-5pm; rest of year: 9:30am-4pm - $25 (ages 2-11 $20).*
😊 It's never a dull moment at the zoo! Almost every half hour, visitors can put questions to the team of zookeepers and help feed the animals. The daily program is handed to you with the entrance ticket. Activities on offer: donkey or camel rides, a carousel, kiddie train, trips in a boat or even a hot-air balloon.

Philadelphia Zoo, modeled on a Victorian pleasure garden, is the oldest zoo in the U.S., opened in 1859. It's home to over 1,300 animals with highlights including, in the **KeyBank Big Cat Falls** section, Amur leopards—named after the Chinese river—, one of the rarest wild cats on the planet, and critically endangered. At the **Rare Animal Conservation Center**, learn all about the animals in need of protection. The **PECO Primate Reserve** providing shelter to various species of monkey is just as fascinating. There's a dedicated area for children where they can learn all about frogs, goats, pigeons, and other more familiar creatures.

Fairmount Park Houses ★

BC1-2-3 *parkcharms.org - opening times vary, please check.*
In the 18th and early 19th-century, Philadelphia's most prosperous residents commissioned country mansions on the cliffs above the Schuylkill River. The seven homes, open to the public, act as time capsules for the interior decor of homes from that era. Worth a mention are the oldest of the lot, **Cedar Grove★** *(1 Cedar Grove Drive)*, a farmhouse built in 1746 from local gray stone, and **Mount Pleasant★** *(3800 Mt Pleasant Drive)*, known for its stunning interior wood paneling.

★ Woodford Mansion – *2300 N. 33rd St. - SEPTA bus no. 32 - ℰ (215) 229 6115 - wood fordmansion.org - guided tours Wed-Sun 10am-4pm - $8 (ages 13-17 $5).* This Georgian-style mansion (1756), subsequently updated by its successive owners, houses a magnificent collection of colonial-style furniture, mostly locally manufactured, and objects patiently collected by Naomi Wood, a philanthropist from Philadelphia.

★ Strawberry Mansion – *2450 Strawberry Mansion Dr. - SEPTA bus no. 32 - ℰ (215) 228 8364 - www. historicstrawberrymansion.org - guided tours Mar-Dec: Wed-Sun 10am-4pm; Feb: Sat 10am-4pm; Jan by appt. only - $8 (-12s free).* From Woodford Mansion, you can walk to the more impressive Strawberry Mansion. Built in the 1780s and originally called "Summerville", it was renamed in 1845 when farmers renting the property served strawberries and cream to the public. Its interior decoration can be described as more eclectic: the kitchen

Scott Spitzer/PHLCVB

Boathouse Row.

is a recreated 18th-century tavern, while the reception room is decked out in furniture acquired in Paris in 1825. On the top floor, two rooms display an intriguing collection of dolls sent to Philadelphia in celebration of the 150th anniversary of the country's independence: there's one representing each state in the Union.

Schuylkill River Trail ★

BC1-2 *30 miles along the Schuylkill River - ☏ (484) 945 0200 - see the cycling routes at www.discoverphl.com.*
Winding through Philadelphia following the Schuylkill River is without a doubt one of the most stunning ways to explore the greater city. On foot or

two wheels, this trail takes you from City Center, through Fairmount Park and as far as Valley Forge, 30 miles away, on a path that is protected most of the way. If you plan to stay just a few days in Philadelphia, opt for the much shorter route across Fairmount Park ⓒ *Philly by Bike, p. 14.*

The Countryside of Philadelphia ★

Just a short trip from Center City (under an hour's drive), The Countryside of Philadelphia is lush with rolling hills, forests and valleys. At its heart, Brandywine Valley and Valley Forge form a string of charming boroughs, historical sites, art venues, farmers markets, and excellent eateries, not to mention some of the largest shopping malls in the country to entice fashion aficionados. The Countryside of Philadelphia is an original and authentic addition to a city break with art, horticulture, rustic walks, and patriotic and historical sites catering to every taste.

▶**Getting there:** The easiest solution is to hire a car. You can reach certain places by train, although this will involve making transfers: the Northeast Regional 052 gets to the Winterthur Museum via Wilmington in 65 minutes. The 002 and 035 train services reach Nemours Estate in an hour. The 104 takes you to West Chester in 70 minutes. The 124, 125 and 139 trains to the King of Prussia Mall and Valley Forge take 40 min. and 65 min. respectively (one train every 20 min.). You can also cycle along the Schuylkill River Trail all the way to Valley Forge (30 miles) (𝄐 p. 62).

Map p. 66.

▶**Tip:** Although The Countryside is near enough to make a round trip from Philadelphia in a day to visit some of its gems, we recommend you spend at least one night in one of the charming towns to truly appreciate the region's allure, gentle way of life, and welcoming locals. For more information, visit: *www.countrysidephl.com*.

BRANDYWINE VALLEY

Longwood Gardens ★★

At Kennett Square (PA), route 1 (30 miles west of Philadelphia, 2 miles north of Wilmington). 1001 Longwood Rd - 𝄐 (610) 388 1000 - longwoodgardens.org - June-Aug: 9am-6pm, Fri-Sat 9am-10pm (opening times vary by season) - $25 (ages 5-18 $13) - themed guided tours (𝄐 see the calendar on the website).

🙂 *The estate puts on events and concerts including the Festival of Fountains, from May to September.*
Pierre S. Du Pont (1870-1954), great grandson of Éleuthère Du Pont, created a horticultural masterpiece while holding two high-powered positions as chairman of the board of both Du Pont and General Motors. Du Pont bought the initial property in 1906, significantly extending it from 200 acres to over 1,000 acres.

Chester County Conference & Visitors Bureau

Longwood Gardens.

★ **Peirce-Du Pont House** – This brick house built by Quaker farmers Joshua and Samuel Peirce (1730) became the Du Pont country pile. Exhibitions and a film retrace the history of the industrialist and his major landscaping endeavors.

Behind the mansion, a footpath takes visitors through the original arboretum to the pristine **Italian Water Garden★★**. In the northwest, the stunning Beaux Arts-style **Conservatory★★** organizes dazzling floral displays that change with the seasons. In summer evenings, **Main Fountain Garden** holds the **Festival of Fountains★★**, a breath-taking symphony of music, light, and dancing jets of water.

Winterthur Museum, Garden & Library ★★★

At Winterthur, route 52 (9 miles south of Longwood Gardens) - ☏ (800) 448 3883 - www.winterthur.org - Tue-Sun 10am-5pm - $20 (ages 2-11 $6) - themed guided tours (☾ check the calendar on the website).

Near Wilmington, this museum of American decorative arts is the former residence of collector **Henry Francis Du Pont** (1880-1969). The Greek Revival building from the 1830s over three stories is the centerpiece of the estate today. The property also features around 1,000 acres of **gardens★** and a preeminent research library.

Take a guided tour of the manor to view the **175 beautifully refurbished rooms★★★** that house Du Pont's rich **decorative arts collection★★★**. Consisting of over 90,000 pieces, this collection of American decorative arts is the largest of its kind with furniture, portraits, and porcelain, tin and silverware objects (1640-1860). The adjoining galleries contain the interactive exhibit **Perspectives on the Decorative Arts in Early America★** (1st floor), and the Winterthur **furniture collection★★** (2nd floor). In the gardens, children will especially appreciate this space designed with youngsters in mind: **Enchanted Woods** (3 acres), with play areas, treehouse, faerie cottage, and more to keep them entertained.

Brandywine Museum of Art ★★

At Chadds Ford (PA), route 1 (28 miles southwest of Philadelphia, 11 miles north of Wilmington) - 1 Hoffman's Mill Rd - ℘ (610) 338 2700 - www.brandywine.org/museum - 9:30am-4:30pm - $18 (ages 6-18 $6).
Set on the banks of the Brandywine Creek, this art museum stands on the site of a gristmill dating from the American Civil War. Celebrated for its collection of paintings by the illustrator **Newell Convers Wyeth** (1882-1945), his son **Andrew Wyeth** (1917-2009), and his grandson **Jamie Wyeth** (born in 1946), the museum also shows, at the **Brandywine Heritage Galleries★** (first floor), artworks by Howard Pyle,

Maxfield Parrish, Charles Dana Gibson, and Rockwell Kent. On the second floor, the **Andrew Wyeth Gallery★★** has a wide selection of paintings spanning the artist's career (*⊙ p. 134*). On fine days, the **beautiful gardens with its river★** surrounding the museum is abloom with local flora. Also open to visitors *(self-guided tour only)* is the family home and studio where N. C. Wyeth lived and worked until his death in 1945. Fascinating too is Andrew Wyeth's studio, originally a school dating from 1875. Andrew Wyeth painted there from 1940 to 2008 and in the house the furniture, library, and collections acquired by the artist have been well preserved. Thousands of pieces by the painter depict the residence and the neighboring countryside.

Hagley Museum and Library ★★

In Wilmington (DE), route 141 (28 miles south of Philadelphia) - 200 Hagley Creek Rd - ℘ (302) 658 2400 - www.hagley.org - Nov to mid-March: 10am-4pm; rest of year: 9am-5pm - $20 (ages 6-14 $10).
On Brandywine's leafy bank, these granite buildings from the early 1800s were part of a vast industrial estate, the world's first producer of gunpowder. Founded in 1802 by French chemist **Éleuthère Irénée Du Pont** (1771-1834), the Hagley gunpowder mill was replaced by the DuPont Company, the world's number one producer of chemicals.

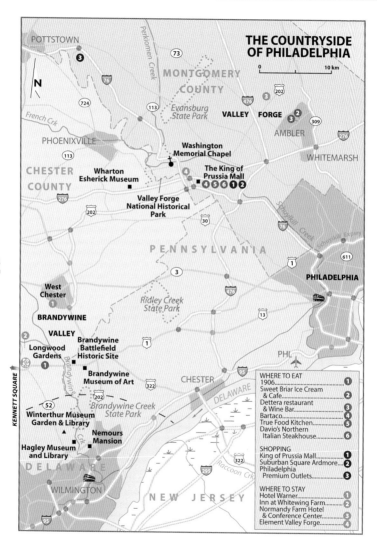

THE COUNTRYSIDE
OF PHILADELPHIA

0   10 km

POTTSTOWN

N

MONTGOMERY
COUNTY

Perkiomen Creek

Evansburg
State Park

VALLEY   FORGE

AMBLER

WHITEMARSH

PHOENIXVILLE

French Crk

CHESTER
COUNTY

Wharton
Esherick Museum

Washington
Memorial Chapel

The King of
Prussia Mall

Valley Forge
National Historical
Park

Schuylkill Expwy

PENNSYLVANIA

West
Chester

Ridley Creek
State Park

PHILADELPHIA

BRANDYWINE

VALLEY

Longwood
Gardens

Brandywine
Battlefield
Historic Site

Brandywine
Museum of Art

Brandywine Creek
State Park

CHESTER

DELAWARE

PHL

KENNETT SQUARE

Winterthur Museum
Garden & Library

Hagley Museum
and Library

Nemours
Mansion

DELAWARE

WILMINGTON

Raccoon Crk

NEW   JERSEY

66

WHERE TO EAT
1906.. ❶
Sweet Briar Ice Cream
& Cafe.. ❷
Dettera restaurant
& Wine Bar..................................... ❸
Bartaco.. ❹
True Food Kitchen....................... ❺
Davio's Northern
Italian Steakhouse...................... ❻

SHOPPING
King of Prussia Mall.................... ❶
Suburban Square Ardmore........ ❷
Philadelphia
Premium Outlets.......................... ❸

WHERE TO STAY
Hotel Warner.................................. ❶
Inn at Whitewing Farm............... ❷
Normandy Farm Hotel
& Conference Center................... ❸
Element Valley Forge.................. ❹

French Alliance Commemoration

The single most important diplomatic success during the American War of Independence was the vital link the colonies fostered with France. The French and American governments signed the Treaty of Alliance in Paris on February 6, 1778. It was this alliance that was a significant contributing factor to the ultimate victory of the American colonies. When news of the Alliance and its ratification by the Continental Congress arrived in Valley Forge in early May 1778, General George Washington issued the following General Order: "It having pleased the Almighty Ruler of the universe to defend the course of the United States, and finally raise up a powerful friend among the princes of the earth, to establish our Liberty and Independence upon a lasting foundation, it becomes us to set apart a day for gratefully acknowledging the Divine goodness, and celebrating the important event which we owe to His Divine interposition."

France's involvement was considerable for the time: tens of thousands of soldiers and 28,000 marines supported the final victory in Yorktown. Five thousand Frenchmen were killed during battle. The cost of this war has been estimated at 12-13 billion euros. A massive debt that proved fatal for the French monarchy and led to the French Revolution.

Every year, on the first weekend in May, the Washington Memorial Chapel commemorates the Treaty of Alliance with France, in line with instructions given by Washington himself.

VALLEY FORGE

Located just over 21 miles from Philadelphia *(around a 35-minute drive)*, the region is known primarily for its eponymous national historical park. Besides Valley Forge National Historical Park that is a fascinating attraction for American history buffs, the valley has an abundance of hiking, bike, and horseback-riding trails suitable for all ages and abilities if you want to explore the great outdoors. Shopping fans will be over the moon to learn that the area is home not only to **Philadelphia Premium Outlets**, where they can snap up great bargains from major American brands, but also the **King of Prussia Mall**, one of the nation's biggest shopping meccas *(☉ p. 97)*. The icing on the cake, purchases are tax free!

Valley Forge National Historical Park ★★

1400 N Outer Line Drive - King of Prussia - ℘ *(610) 783 1000 - www.nps. gov/vafo/index.htm - admission free.* This national historical park is a source of pride for the region. Whether you're a patriot, American history enthusiast, or inquisitive traveler, a visit to this park gives you a quick lesson on the immense suffering that George Washington and his troops endured one winter while the British army occupied Philadelphia. The site is a journey back in time to the winter encampment of 1777-1778 when the Continental Army composed of Thirteen American Colonies and led by the first President of the United States fought the British Empire in the battle for independence. While no confrontation took place in Valley Forge, it was a strategic site, and the encampment was one of the most grueling periods of the American War of Independence.

The brand new **Visitor Center** has a chronological exhibition alongside objects and artefacts that make for an enlightening introduction to the park. You can explore the park by yourself or ride a trolley in small groups with a local guide. Visitors can discover the **National Arch Memorial** commemorating the arrival of George Washington and his army, as well as the **Patriots of African Descent Monument**, honoring the contributions of African Americans in the American Revolution. The house serving as Washington's Headquarters and the log cabins inhabited by soldiers are a reminder of the harsh encampment conditions. Historic reconstructions are put on all year round by volunteers in period dress.

Washington Memorial Chapel

Located in Valley Forge NHP, on Valley Forge Road (Route 23), just over 1 mile from the Visitor Center - ☏ (610) 783 0120 - wmchapel.org.
This Gothic Revival-style chapel was built between 1903 and 1917 for two purposes: to honor George Washington and serve the Episcopal needs of the local area. Located on the road that traverses the National Historical Park, it is frequented as much by regular parishoners as tourists. Its tower houses the **Justice Bell**, a replica of the Liberty Bell, which toured Pennsylvania between 1915 and 1920 and became an instrumental symbol of the Women's Suffrage movement. Containing 58 bronze bells, its carillon is one of the largest in the world and weighs in at 26 tons. The Veterans Wall of Honor immortalizes American servicemen and women, living or dead.

71

ADDRESSES

73

Geno's Steaks.
ferrantraite/Getty Images Plus

Where to Eat

Philadelphia has an incredible food scene and has nothing to feel self-conscious about next to its arguably more famous neighbors. From the iconic Philly cheesesteak, devoured on the move, to award-winning eateries, the city offers many mouth-watering reasons for foodies to make a beeline for Philly. Weekend brunch and happy hours are Philly institutions—and great opportunities to mix with the locals.

Every type of cuisine is on offer, although it would be a shame to leave without trying a local specialty or two. **Crabfries** are crinkle-cut French fries sprinkled with a secret blend of spices and a creamy cheese sauce. The **Philly cheesesteak** is thinly sliced ribeye beef and melted cheese served warm on a long bread roll—with grilled onions and mushrooms on top if you're not a cheesesteak purist. Reserved for those with a strong constitution, the **Twinkie Burger** is a cheese-and-bacon burger sandwiched between deep-fried Twinkies.

Philadelphia's **Chinatown (F4)** hasn't broken the mold. It's a goldmine for tasty places to eat, for every pocket, even the most modest.

Food trucks – *roaminghunger.com.* As in New York, Baltimore and plenty of other cities, food trucks serve up a host of varied and excellent fast-food fare at lunchtime. An experience not to be missed!

😊 Check out the **Food & Drink** menu option on the **discoverphl.com** website, which has a section on New Restaurants: **www.discoverphl.com/dine**.

☌ Find the addresses on our maps using the numbers on the listing (e.g. ❶). The **coordinates in red** (e.g. **C2**) refer to the detachable map (inside the cover).

OLD CITY, SOCIETY HILL & PENN'S LANDING

Old City

Local Map p. 26.

On the Go

㊺ The Bourse Food Hall – G5 - *111 S. Independence Mall E.* - ℘ *(215) 625 0300* - *theboursephilly.com* - *Mon-Sat 7am-10pm, Sun 9am-6pm.* This splendid building from the early 19th century, beautifully restored, was once a stock exchange, maritime exchange, and grain-trading center. It's since been converted into a food hall with a dozen vendors serving internationally inspired cuisine with strong local roots. Plenty to choose from!

Under $20

㉑ Sonny's – G5 - *228 Market St.* - ℘ *(215) 629 5760* - *www.sonnyscheesesteaks*.

com - 11am-110pm - $10-20. A five-minute walk from Independence Hall, Sonny's serves up the city's iconic cheesesteak. The multi-award-winning classic cheesesteak is the most authentic—or have it with bacon or chicken, or even gluten-free! Cheeseburgers, BBQ burgers, and vegetarian options also on the menu.

㉓ Campo's – G5 - 214 Market St. - ✆ (215) 923 1000 - www.camposdeli. com - 9:30am-10pm - $10-20. Just doors down from its neighbor, Campo's is a Philly institution and its cheesesteak is the official cheesesteak of the Philadelphia Phillies, the city's baseball team! It was founded in 1947 by an Italian family, and the recipes have been handed down through the generations. In addition, choose from sandwiches, house salads, Italian deli cold cuts, and a selection of craft beers.

$20-40

㉖ Fork – G5 - 306 Market St. - ✆ (215) 625 9425 - www. forkrestaurant.com - 11am-9pm, Fri-Sat 11am-10pm - closed Mon - mains $19-36. Well known in foodie circles, this restaurant spotlights local produce, mostly organic and always seasonal. The reasonably portioned dishes tend towards Mediterranean flavors, while the cuisine is elevated but never pretentious, just like the ambience and interior. The weekend brunch is popular so booking is advised.

㉔ Positano Coast – G5 - 212 Walnut St., 2nd floor - ✆ (215) 238 0499 - www.positanocoast.net - Tue-Sun

11:30am-9pm, closed Mon - $20-40. Within walking distance from Independence Hall and the Museum of the American Revolution, Positano Coast is ideal for a meal before or after your history tour. The restaurant is on the 2nd floor of a building shaped like a ship's bow. In warm weather, sit out on the terrace overlooking the Greek Revival building housing the Merchants' Exchange with its colonnaded rotunda. As its name suggests, the cuisine is inspired by Italy—the Amalfi Coast to be precise. Seafood therefore features heavily on the menu, from grilled octopus and seafood risotto to sea urchin linguine and lobster ravioli. Meat lovers will also find veal parmigiana and even a burger.

㉘ Amada – G5 - 217-219 Chestnut St. - ✆ (215) 625 2450 - amadarestaurant. com - Mon-Fri 5pm-10pm, Sat-Sun 4pm-10pm, brunch Sat-Sun 11:30am-3pm - tapas, plantxas, plates $10-26, paella to share $49. With its hanging *jamòns* and wooden counter, Amada checks every box of the typical Spanish *bodega* revisited in a New England style. Its owner, the chef **Jose Garces**, is a star on the East Coast culinary scene, after winning the prestigious Best Chef, Mid-Atlantic Award and the coveted title of *Iron Chef*. Treat your taste buds to *gambas al ajillo* (garlic shrimp), delicious platxas of Iberian cold cuts, or *croquetas de Bacalao* (cod fritters). The dining room can get pretty noisy, so try to get a table on the terrace when the weather is playing ball.

75

Over $60

💙 **25** **Zahav – G5** - *237 St. James Pl. - ☎ (215) 625 8800 - www.zahavrestaurant.com - 5pm-9:30pm - closed Sun-Mon - tasting menu $75 reservation only.* The man who introduced Israeli cuisine to Philadelphia, chef **Michael Solomonov** (☞ *p. 18*) has made Zahav the go-to destination for anyone looking to explore the delicate flavors of the Middle East. Inside, the decor subtly references the Mahane Yehuda "shuk", the traditional market in Jerusalem, but the inked kitchen team soon remind you that you are well and truly in Philadelphia! Zahav, whose reputation is now international, serves mouth-watering and hearty dishes, in keeping with Michael Solomonov's desire to share the culinary delights of his home country. And share them he does with a seasonal menu that is a journey through the senses, transporting us in a matter of mouthfuls from Philly to Jerusalem.

Society Hill & Penn's Landing

Local Map p. 26

On the Go

22 **Ishkabibble's – G6** - *517 S St. - ☎ (215) 922 0494 - www.eatishkabibbles.com - Sun-Thu 9:30am-11pm, Fri-Sat 9:30am-midnight - $10-20.* More **cheesesteaks**, yes, but this is the home of the chicken cheesesteak, created here in 1979. Another original take on this iconic sandwich: the South Philly Cheesesteak topped with roasted peppers, sauteed spinach, and provolone cheese.

$20-40

27 **Bloomsday Café – G6** - *414 S 2nd St. - ☎ (267) 319 8018 - www.bloomsdaycafe.com - Wed-Sat 5pm-9pm, brunch Fri-Sun 10am-2pm - brunch $22-35, dinner $25-40.* This warm and welcoming spot serving seasonal cuisine is frequented by locals, which is always a good sign. The varied menu has Mediterranean and French influences and priority is given to fresh, local, and organic ingredients. Excellent beer and wine list. In warmer months, the patio offers al fresco dining across from, every Sunday, Headhouse Farmers' Market (☞ *p. 94*).

$40-65

29 **Moshulu – G6** - *401 S Christopher Columbus Blvd - ☎ (215) 923 2500 - www.moshulu.com - Mon-Thu 4pm-9pm, Fri 4pm-10pm, Sat 10am-10pm, Sun 10am-8pm and brunch Sat-Sun till 3pm - $30-65.* Looking for a unique dining experience? Then board the *Moshulu*, a splendid four-masted ship moored in Penn's Landing. Built in Scotland in 1904 for a German shipping company, the steel barque was seized by the U.S. during World War I. After a life on the open seas, it finally cast anchor on the Delaware, where it affords beautiful views of the river, the *USS Olympia* cruiser (1895), the *USS Becuna* submarine (1944), and the state of New Jersey across the water. Ideal for a cocktail on the deck or a romantic dinner in the hold. The dishes are generous and excellent: seafood platters, orecchiette crab, stuffed whole lobster, and plancha seared swordfish, to name a few.

Fishtown

Detachable Map

On the Go

32 Joe's Steaks + Soda Shop – G2 - 1 W Girard Ave. - ☎ (215) 423 5637 - www.joessteaks.com - 11am-9pm, Fri-Sat 11am-midnight - $10-20. Following the first location opened in 1949 in the Tacony district, a blue-collar and immigrant neighborhood, this new address continues to serve the cheesesteaks, burgers, sandwiches, and milkshakes that made it popular.

Under $20

36 Sancho Pistolas – G2 - 19 W Girard Ave. - ☎ (267) 324 3530 - www.pistolaslife.com - 11:30am-2am - $15-20. A bar and restaurant serving Mexican snacks, dishes, and cocktails. The eclectic mix of patrons comes for the guacamole, tacos, nachos, beers and tequilas, in an atmosphere that is always buzzy.

$20-40

37 LMNO – G1 - 1739-1749 N Front St. - ☎ (215) 770 7001 - www.lmnophilly. com - Mon-Thu 4pm-10pm, Fri 5pm-11pm, Sat 10am-3pm, 5pm-11pm, Sun 10am-3pm, 5pm-10pm - $20-35, large dishes to share $65. Hip Latin venue with modern and enticing decor. The menu of Mexican and South American dishes features the main classics: tacos, tostados, and ceviches. The dishes are rich in color and flavor. Creative cocktails and an impressive selection of liquors, with tequilas and mezcals top of the list. Attractive patio.

$40-60

❤ **34 Izakaya by Yanaga – H1** - 1832 Frankford Ave. - ☎ (267) 310 3554 - www.byyanaga.com - Mon-Thu 4pm-10pm, Fri-Sat 4pm-11pm, Sun 2pm-9pm - $20-35, sharing $55-75. An elegant and contemporary Japanese restaurant serving delicate sushi, sashimi, maki, rolls, and ramen, which you can wash down with a wide choice of sakes, beers, and wines. Tapas style portions perfect for ordering through your sitting, or larger plates to split. Attracts Fishtown's friendly hipster crowd.

Alcohol

The alcohol laws in Philadelphia are some of the country's strictest, and it is against the law to sell alcohol to anyone under 21 years of age. If you have young people with you, you will often be asked to show ID.

Bring Your Own Bottle

Another particularity of the city, alcohol licenses are prohibitively expensive for many independent restaurants. Consequently, plenty of them have a BYOB policy so patrons can bring their own bottle. What feels like a hassle is actually a godsend given the exorbitant drinks prices in some venues. Enquire with the restaurant before rocking up with a bottle.

㉟ Suraya Cafe Market Restaurant & Garden – *G1* - *1528 Frankford Ave. - ℘ (215) 302 1900 - www.surayaphilly.com - lunch $25, brunch $40, dinner $45-60.* Named after the owners' beloved grandmother, this restaurant is a tribute to Lebanese cuisine, fusing Levantine family specialties with world flavors. Expect to find hummous, taboulé, and marinated chicken alongside New Zealand shrimp and American ribeye steak. Extensive selection of Lebanese wines and araks. It's especially nice dining in the pretty rear patio and garden, open from April to October.

Kensington

Detachable Map

78

$20-30

㉝ Eeva – *G1* - *310 W Master - ℘(267) 687 7910 - www.eevaphilly. com - Thu-Sat 5pm-9:30pm, Sun 4pm-9pm, bakery daily 8am-3pm - $19-30*. Located in historic Olde Kensington, in the throes of regeneration, this address is a relative newcomer but already popular with locals, digital nomads, and the executive crowd. The weekly changing menu is simple but packed with flavor and made using locally sourced ingredients. Feast on fresh salads and delicious artisanal pizzas. The wine list includes natural wines, consciously selected by the chef and his partner. The bakery counter serves a tasty selection of breads and rolls.

CENTER CITY & WASHINGTON SQUARE

Center City

Local Map p. 40.

On the Go

❶ Reading Terminal Market – *F4* - *N. 12th St. and Arch St. - Center City - ℘ (215) 922 2317 - www.readingterminalmarket.org -* 🅿 *prices vary by merchant - 8am-6pm.* The market is home to countless stalls for eating on the fly. The most famous include: DiNic's for its roast pork sandwich and Pearl's Oyster Bar its delectable mussels in white wine. Vegans should make a beeline for Luhv while Down Home Diner serves up an all-American breakfast.

Under $20

❷ McGillin's Olde Ale House – *E5* - *1310 Drury St. - Center City - ℘ (215) 735 5562 - mcgillins. com - midday-2am, Mon 4pm-2am - mains under $15*. One of the oldest Irish pubs in Philly, established in 1860, has kept its authenticity and charm. The beer is always flowing, and the menu is tasty and varied. On the weekend, the venue is full to bursting, ditto on match days and St. Patrick's Day.

$20-40

⓭ XIX Nineteen – *E5* - *200 S Broad St. - 19th floor - ℘ (215) 790 1919 - www.nineteenrestaurant.com - bar and lounge - dinner Tue-Sat 3pm-midnight - $20-35*. On the

19th story of the historic **The Bellevue** Hotel, the restaurant and lounge of this venue is set under a stunning rotunda. With sweeping views of the city, the place serves breakfast and brunch too. Head to the lounge to sample their list of wines, cocktails, and other beverages for happy hour or pre dinner. The cozy and intimate bar is perfect for a catch-up with friends or a date.

Chinatown

Local Map p. 40.

Under $20

④ **Penang – F4** - 117 N 10th St. - ℘ (215) 413 2531 - penangphilly.com - 11:30am-9:30pm, Fri-Sun 11am-11pm - appetizers $6-10, noodles and mains $11-19. Penang offers a taste of Malaysia in Philly. The dishes are hearty and full of flavor, whether you like it hot or not, and vegetarians are well catered for. Fans of satay chicken and fried noodles won't be disappointed. Service is snappy even during the lunch rush.

$20-30

③ **Dim Sum Garden – F4** - 1020 Race St. - ℘ (215) 873 0258 - www.dimsumgardenphilly.com - 11am-10pm - $19-27. Locals especially flock to this eatery opened in 2013 for its steamed dumplings. The menu features other Shanghai specialties made with vegetables, fish, seafood, or meat. Smoothies and bubble teas make an unexpected but welcome sweet option.

Washington Square

Local Map p. 40.

Over $40

♥ ⑤ **Talula's Garden – F5** - 210 W Washington Square - ℘ (215) 592 7787 - www.talulasgarden.com - 5pm-10pm, Fri-Sat 4pm-10pm, Sun 10am-2pm, 4pm-10pm - appetizers and boards $15-25, mains $34-50 - reservation only. As green and delightful as its name suggests, this farmhouse-chic eatery showcases the best of farm-to-fork eating so championed by its chef Aimee Olexy. The seasonal menu is composed of locally sourced ingredients. From the appetizers through dessert, the dishes are harmonious in flavor and color, offering a feast for both the eyes and palate. An enchanted garden in the heart of Philly.

Midtown/Gayborhood

Local Map p. 40.

Under $15

⑧ **Masala Kitchen – F5** - 1115 Walnut St. - ℘ (215) 309 3301 - www.masalakitchenphilly.com - Mon-Thu 11am-midnight, Fri 11am-3:30am, Sat midday-3:30am, Sun midday-11pm - mains under $15. Cantine serving typically Indian street food. Naan breads and kati rolls or bowls of chicken biryani are made to perfection. Selection of vegetarian options.

$20-30

♥ ⑪ **Grandma's Philly – EF5** - 1304 Walnut St. - ℘ (215) 315 9050 -

79

www.grandmasphilly.com -
11:30am-10:30pm, Fri-Sun midday-
11pm, closed Wed - soups, salads,
small plates under $15, main $16-25.
Traditional fragrant Thai dishes served
tapas style to share (or not!) made like
Grandma used to make. Open since
2022, this eatery favors fresh, local
produce.

9 **Green Eggs Café – EF5** -
1301 Locust St. - ℘ (267) 861 0314 -
www.greeneggscafe.com - 9am-3pm,
Sat-Sun 9am-4pm - $25-30, cash
payment only. American classics
(pancakes, waffles, eggs) in generous
portions. The crème brûlée-style French
toast and the Steak & Eggs get special
mentions. Immensely popular for
brunch at weekends, expect a long wait.

7 **Prunella – F5** - 112 S 13th St. -
℘ (215) 631 8058 - www.prunellaphl.
com - 11:30am-10pm, Fri-Sat
11:30am-midnight - mains $16-22,
pizzas $17. This Italian eatery serves
elevated Italian in a gorgeous setting.
Enjoy appetizing pizzas with original
names and beautifully presented
dishes made using fresh, seasonal
ingredients.

Over $40

15 **Vedge – F5** - 1221 Locust St. -
℘ (215) 320 7500 -
www.vedgerestaurant.com -
5pm-9pm, closed Sun-Mon - dinner
$45-65. Set in a period house, this
restaurant with cozy vibes offers a
creative menu exclusively made with
seasonal veggies, locally sourced as
much as possible. Vegan ingredients
are elevated to stratospheric heights

and are sure to convert even the
most voracious meat-eater! Inventive
cocktails and selective wine list.

Passyunk Square & Italian Market

Detachable Map

On the Go

31 **Geno's – F7** - 1219 S 9th St. -
℘ (215) 389 0659 - www.genossteaks.
com - 24/7 - $12-19. Its vintage neon
sign has lit up a corner between Italian
Market and Passyunk since 1966. A
family affair and local institution as
far as cheesesteaks and sandwiches
go, Geno's always attracts a crowd!
Its popularity has spawned a range of
T-shirts, mugs, and other souvenirs.

Under $20

♥ **42** **P'unk Burger – F8** -
1823 Passyunk Ave - ℘ (215) 468
7865 - www.punkburger.com -
Mon-Thu 11am-10pm, Fri-Sat
10am-midnight, Sun 10am-10pm -
$14-20. A burger joint not like any
other. All the patties and hot dogs are
made from organic and humanely-
raised meat, free from antibiotics,
pesticides, and hormones. Seafood
is wild-caught. All other ingredients
and the drinks are sourced from local
fairtrade producers. There's a burger
for every taste, from healthy to fully
loaded. Enjoy with a side of sweet
potato fries or tater tots. Vegetarian,
vegan, and gluten-free options.
Desserts include milkshakes and ice
creams from vendors such as **The
Franklin Fountain** (ℂ p. 89).

$20-40

💜 **30** **Casa Mexico** – **F7** - *1134 S 9th St. (Italian Market)* - ℘ *(267) 470 1464* - *www.casamexicophl.com* - *10am-10pm - $18-30.* A restaurant with a whole lot of soul. All down to **Cristina Martinez**, a generous and humble culinary personality, winner of the prestigious James Beard Award for Best Chef, Mid-Atlantic, in 2022. A Mexican immigrant who arrived in the U.S. undocumented, Cristina is the embodiment of the American Dream. Her papers in order, she and her husband began selling authentic tacos from a pushcart outside their Philadelphia home. On the back of this success, she opened her own place, **South Philly Barbacoa**, in the Italian Market, a hub for the city's immigrant population, instantly attracting foodies from all over the city and the country, as proved by the long wait lines! Cristina then opened on the same block Casa Mexico, in homage to her native roots. Everything is homemade and portions are generous. Choose from mouth-watering tacos to house specialties like Red Mole Chicken, or quesadillas stuffed with fresh ingredients and melt-in-the-mouth meat. End on a sweet note with the Tres Leches cake. A welcome additional feather in Philly's culinary cap.

43 **Gabriella's Vietnam** – **F8** - *1837 E Passyunk Ave* - ℘ *(272) 888 3298* - *www.gabriellasvietnam.com* - *5pm-10pm, Sun 4pm-8:30pm, closed Mon - $22-39.* An authentically Vietnamese restaurant. A Saigon native, the chef Than Nguyen pays tribute to her family's culinary heritage and Vietnamese street food. The ingredients are handpicked by the chef from the city's local farmers' markets. Anyone familiar with Vietnamese cuisine will spot classics like beef loc lac, lemongrass and shrimp fried rice, and dumplings wrapped in banana leaves. Delicious!

$40-60

44 **Mish Mish** – **F8** - *1046 Tasker St.* - ℘ *(267) 761 9750* - *www.mishmishphilly.com* - *Thu-Mon 5pm-10pm - $43-60.* Right in the heart of Passyunk, this address has casual chic down to a tee. Conversation flows easily amidst the stylish and minimalist interior. Appealing plates of food are made to share and the at times unexpected combinations of flavors are a treat for the taste buds from appetizers through dessert. The servers are attentive and cheerful. A lovely dining experience.

BENJAMIN FRANKLIN PARKWAY & RITTENHOUSE SQUARE

Benjamin Franklin Parkway

Local Map p. 40.

Over $40

12 **Urban Farmer** – **E4** - *1850 Benjamin Franklin Pkwy* - ℘ *(215) 963 2788* - *www.urbanfarmersteakhouse.com* - *8am-2pm, 4pm-11pm, Sun 8am-2pm, 4pm-10pm - brunch and lunch $30-45,* *dinner $50-75*. A modern steakhouse serving up cuts from the best ranches locally and nationally. The steak tasting plate comes with three steaks, one of which is aged. For brunch, the dishes feature seafood and shellfish from local fishers, and eggs and veggies supplied straight from farm to table.

Over $60

❤ **16** **Vernick Fish** – **E4** - *1 N 19th St. - ℘ (215) 419 5055 - www.vernickfish. com - 5pm-10pm, closed Sun-Tue - oysters and appetizers $20-25, mains $35-115 - reservation only.*
The traditional oyster bar is here revisited with elegance and contemporary style by the chef **Greg Vernick**. The open kitchen, modern interior, and fun and fashionable crowd contribute to the glamorous look and feel of the place. All the fish and shellfish are sourced from fairtrade and sustainable suppliers and ingredients from responsible farmers. Purists will appreciate the platters of oysters caught daily and the delicate flavors of the tartares and ceviches. The dishes with elevated flavor combinations are a treat for the senses. One of the best fish restaurants in the city.

Over $100

20 **Jean-Georges Philadelphia** – **E4** - *1 N 19th St. (Four Seasons Hotel Philadelphia at Comcast Center) - ℘(215) 419 5057 - www.jean-georgesphiladelphia. com - Thu-Sat 5:30pm-9:30pm - Two 6-course tasting menus: $198 for the vegetarian and $218 for fish & meat - reservation only.* Dinner at Jean-Georges is a complete experience that begins the moment you board the elevator. The car shoots up to the 60th story of the Four Seasons Philadelphia in under a minute as the whole of Philadelphia flashes by. At 1,121 feet tall, the glass and steel tower, the tallest in Pennsylvania and designed by Norman Foster, practically brushes the clouds. Your arrival in the lobby is spectacular, as much for the Norman Foster-designed black marble decor and floral displays as the panoramic views. It's the same level of Insta-worthy style in the dining room, awash with glass and mirrors overlooking the city far down below. At the helm of the restaurant headed by Michelin-starred New York chef **Jean-Georges Vongerichten** is a young German chef, **Cornelia Sühr**, who honed her craft in Alain Ducasse's kitchens. Cornelia, an enthusiastic pianist in her down time, applies the same deft touch and precision to her cooking, such as in Jean-Georges' signature dishes: egg toast caviar with herbs, and yellowfin tuna noodles, avocado, ginger dressing, and radish. But also in new compositions written in duet with Jean-Georges and inspired by Pennsylvania's farmers, like the roasted cod, hazelnut-anise emulsion, and broccoli rabe, or golden ossestra caviar meyer lemon gelée and crème fraiche. Subtle pairings of flavors producing a culinary symphony that will stay with you forever.

Rittenhouse Square

Local Map p. 40.

On the Go

46 Di Bruno Bros – E5 - *1730 Chestnut St. - Rittenhouse Square - ℘ (215) 665 9220 - www.dibruno. com - Mon-Sat 7am-9pm, Sun 7am-7pm.* Temptations are everywhere you look in this purveyor of fine Italian foods, one of five vendors that all started at the Italian Market in 1939 (**☞** *p. 96*)! Take-out sandwiches and other dishes, a counter for breakfast or afternoon tea, and a small restaurant. It's all delicious.

Under $20

♥ **10 K'far Cafe – E5** - *110 S 19th St. - ℘ (267) 800 7200 - www.kfarcafe. com - 8am-5pm, closed Mon-Tue - brunch and lunch $20.* Retro-chic decor and nice vibes. A go-to destination for breakfast and brunch, this cafe is famed for its yummy Israeli and Middle Eastern specialties, concocted by the talented **Michael Solomonov** (**☞** *p. 18*). While the Jerusalem bagels, *borekas* (stuffed pastries) and Friday's challah bread are showstoppers, the pastries, toast, and bowls are equally satisfying. A special mention to the *kubaneh toast*, which,

K. Huff/PHLCVB

Philly cheesesteak.

sweet or savory, is simply divine. A feel good place that will have you coming back for more.

6 Revolution Taco – D5 - *2015 Walnut St. - ☏ (267) 639 5681 - www.therevolutiontaco.com - 11am-8:30pm, closed Sun - tacos and burritos $11-15, empanadas and dessert $4-6.* This counter-serve taqueria wears its ambition to revolutionize the humble taco on its sleeve. Here the understated taco is homemade and served in the traditional way: small corn taco shells (almost all gluten-free) with a selection of mouth-watering fillings. The modern approach fuses Mexican flavors with Asian or Texan notes such as Korean Beef, Salsa Verde Chicken, and BBQ Mushroom tacos. Opt for the delicious espresso-flavored churros for dessert.

$20-40

14 Veda - *1920 Chestnut St. - E5 - ☏ (267) 519 2001 - www.vedaphilly.com - 11:30am-2:30pm, 4:30pm-9:30pm - lunch $17-22, dinner $22-30.* This bistro-style restaurant serves Indian cuisine with a modern twist. The presentation is impeccable and the dishes are rich in flavors and colors. Hands down one of the top Indian eateries in Philadelphia.

17 Oyster House – E5 - *1516 Sansom St. - ☏ (215) 567 7683 - www.oysterhousephilly.com - 11:30am-9pm Tue-Thu, 11:30am-10pm Fri-Sat, closed Sun-Mon - oysters, soups, salads $12-24, sandwiches, mains $18-40.* A Philly icon, this oyster bar opened in 1947 has been passed down from father to son over three generations. The menu features oysters predominantly sourced from the U.S. East Coast along with a selection of American shellfish and seafood specialties such as crab cakes, lobster rolls, and clam chowders. If the day's catch is successful, the Maine lobster is served whole and grilled (*around $60*).

$40-50

19 The Love – E5 - *130 S. 18th St. - Rittenhouse Square - ☏ (215) 433 1555 - theloverestaurant. com - Mon-Fri 11:30am-2pm, 5pm-10pm, Sat-Sun 10am-2pm, 5pm-10pm - mains $27-48.* This eatery was established by two darlings of North American fine dining: **Aimee Olexy**, at the helm of the must-go Talula's Table (*☛ p. 87*), and **Stephen Starr**, owner of several restaurants in the U.S. and overseas. The Love has a dining room with exposed brick walls and warm decor, the ideal setting for a refined yet relaxed culinary experience. The dishes lean towards local produce as much as possible. The menu is seasonal and an absolute delight for lovers of innovative flavors. The carrot cake on the dessert menu is amazing.

Over $60

♥ 18 Her Place Supper Club – E5 - *1740 Sansom St. - www.herplacephilly.com - Tue-Fri Two seatings: 6pm and 8:30pm - reservation only at www.exploretock. com/herplace and 2 people*

Amanda Shulman, Her Place Supper Club.

min. - different menu every two weeks, hence why reservations are released every other Sunday. View the menu on Instagram: @herplacesupperclub - set menu $85. It's a leading light of the current food scene and with just 24 covers, booking well in advance is a must if you want to experience one of Philadelphia's hottest fine dining destinations. A political science graduate, **Amanda Shulman**, 29, wasn't predestined to becoming a chef, despite it being a family tradition. A tradition that ultimately took precedence over her studies, her tiny campus apartment transformed into a restaurant for a community of foodies. Her vocation was decided. Amanda went on to learn from some of the

greatest North American chefs, spent a year in Bergamo studying Italian cuisine, then discovered French cuisine in Montreal alongside her Quebecer fiancé. A revelation! Her French-Italian cooking is peppered with Jewish influences. Every evening, she serves a six-course meal, as Amanda explains in person to all her guests. All the produce is organic and locally sourced, down to the caviar from New England.

Over $100

41 **Friday Saturday Sunday** – **D5** - *261 S 21st St. - ☏ (215) 546 4232 - www.fridaysaturdaysunday.com - Wed-Sun 5pm-11pm - 8-course tasting menu $150, reservation only.* A restaurant set in a historic two-story residence with a first floor bar that is often packed with cool 30- and 40-somethings come to soak up the friendly vibes. Diners must head upstairs to the effortlessly chic Art Nouveau dining room. The seasonal menu is an indulgent eight courses of elevated, innovative or revisited dishes. Vegetables, pasta, fish, meat, desserts… the combinations of aromas, flavors, and textures are at once familiar yet uncharted. Fine dining at its most masterful.

University City

Local Map p. 40
and Detachable Map

On the Go

40 **Pita Chip** – **C5** - *3601 Market St. - ☏ (215) 397 4251 - www. pitachipphilly.com - 11am-8pm,*

K. Huff/PHLCVB

86

Louie Louie.

Sat-Sun 11am-6pm - $13-20. With a constant stream of students from the neighborhood passing through the door, this fast-casual eatery serves modern Middle Eastern-inspired street food. Bowls of rice, marinated meats, fresh salads, hummous, falafels, wraps, chicken shawarmas, and baklavas for dessert—they've got it covered. Excellent value for money.

$20-40

💙 38 **White Dog Cafe** – **C5** - *3420 Sansom St. - ☏ (215) 386 9224 - www.whitedog.com - 11am-9pm, Sat 9am-9pm, Sun 9am-8pm - lunch, vegetarian menu, and brunch $19-40, dinner $25-60.* This venue occupying a trio of Victorian brownstones features whimsical dog decor adorning the various dining spaces. It was the first restaurant to adopt the farm to table concept when it opened in Philly 40 years ago and only uses local, mostly organic, foods. Today, the chef is proud to carry on this philosophy, sourcing everything from local farms within a 50-mile radius. A second, exclusively veggie, menu, devised by the chef, is also available.

$40-60

39 **Louie Louie** – **C5** - *3611 Walnut St. - ☏ (267) 805 8585 - www.louielouie. restaurant - 11am-9pm, Sat 10am-9pm, Sun 10am-8pm - lunch and brunch $30-50, dinner $40-65.* With Art Deco decor, comfy booths, and vintage

dining furniture, this venue oozes Parisian vibes. The menu adds to the bistro ambience with oysters, onion soup gratinée, brie & pear salad, steak frites, and profiteroles all featured. If it wasn't for the juicy burger, smashed avocado on toast, and Caesar salad, you'd almost forget you were in Philly!

THE COUNTRYSIDE OF PHILADELPHIA

Map p. 66.

Kennett Square

$25-50

❤ **Portabellos of Kennett Square** – **Off map** – 108 State St. - ℘ (610) 925 4984 - www.portabellosofkennettsquare.com - Wed-Thu 4pm-8pm, Fri 4pm-9pm, Sat midday-9pm, Sun midday-8pm - brunch $25-35, dinner $30-50. Chef Brett and his wife Sandra have just celebrated 10 years running this hospitable establishment. Friendly service and delicious, generous Italian-influenced cuisine where the humble mushroom, champion of the borough and the state, is the star of the show. The roasted mushroom soup is sublime. That said, the pizzas, pastas, steaks, and fish dishes are just as appetizing!

1906 – Longwood Gardens, 1001 Longwood Road, Kennett Square - ℘ (610) 388 5290 - longwoodgardens.org/dine/1906 - lunch 11:30am-2:30pm, seasonal opening times, enquire - $33-50.

Set in the lush gardens, the restaurant decked out in wooden furniture and hanging plants resembles a beautiful conservatory. Dishes featuring seasonal ingredients with botanical and floral garnishes are just as good to look at as they are to eat.

Over $120

Talula's Table – **Off Map** – 102 W State St. - ℘ (610) 444 8255 - www.talulastable.com - cafe 7am-6pm, dinner 7pm-11pm - cafe $20-35, dinner tasting menu $125 - reservation only. Foodies across the country are talking about it. By day, Talula's Table is a gourmet cafe and market stocked with local organic foods; by night, the venue is an artisanal destination dinner experience featuring carefully selected ingredients that will satisfy the most discerning palate. Two tables, around 20 covers, and an elaborate eight-course menu. A wonderfully memorable culinary experience, under the auspices of **Aimee Olexy**, the chef who also established Talula's Garden in Philadelphia (**☞** p. 79). Two successes to her name worth celebrating.

Ambler

$10-25

② **Sweet Briar Ice Cream & Cafe** – 11 Lindelwold Ave. - ℘ (215) 542 0272 - www.sweetbriar.net - 8am-9pm, Sun-Mon 8am-2pm - lunch $10-19, dinner $20-25. A quaint typically American cafe popular with families and regulars. From breakfast to dinner, the menu has pancakes, omelets,

87

burgers, sandwiches, meatballs, and other classics.

$30-50

❸ Dettera Restaurant & Wine Bar – *129 East Butler Ave. - ☎ (215) 643 0111 - www.deterra.com - Tue-Sat 4pm-9pm - $31-50.* Upscale eatery and wine bar serving a New American menu with Italian influences. Frequented by sophisticated locals who come for date nights or to sample the excellent wines, cheeses, and cold cuts.

King of Prussia

$20-30

❹ Bartaco – *160 N. Gulph Road, suite C110 - ☎ (610) 510 8226 - www.bartaco.com - 11am-9pm, Sun 11am-10pm, Mon-Thu 11am-11pm - $20-30 - card payments only.* Take a break from shopping at Bartaco serving up burgers, pizzas and other fast food options. Inspired by Brazilian and Californian beach culture, the fare here is upscale street food based around fusion tacos packed with aromatic herbs—so fresh, spicy, tasty, and healthy all at once. Also enjoy freshly pressed fruit juices, cocktails, and

88

beers. Provided you don't overindulge, the check is usually reasonable. The concept is so successful, Bartaco has over 20 locations in the U.S.

❺ True Food Kitchen – *239 Mall Boulevard - ☎ (484) 751 1954 - www.truefoodkitchen.com - 11am-9pm, Sat 10am-10pm, Sun 10am-9pm - $20-29.* An eco-chic chain serving health-conscious dishes suitable for all ages with a children's menu and a wide selection of balanced and appetizing fare. Enjoy fresh fruit juices and beverages during your meal and fairtrade coffees and teas to wrap it up. Healthy and delicious.

$30-60

❻ Davio's Northern Italian Steakhouse – *200 Main St. - King of Prussia - ☎ (610) 337 4810 - www.davios.com - Mon-Thu 11:30am-10pm, Fri 11:30am-11pm, Sun 11am-10pm - brunch/lunch $30-45, dinner $40-65.* Fine Italian dining with a full range of seafood, antipasti, pizzas, pastas, fish, and desserts. The portions are as generous as you'd expect, and the wine list is decent. Enjoy al fresco dining on the patio in warm weather.

Where to Drink

Philadelphia has a long **beer** tradition, and even has its own festival devoted to the malted beverage (◐ *Festivals and Events p. 119*). There are several craft breweries in Philly, one of the best known being **Yards**.

In recent years, the bar scene in Philly has flourished and the city has plenty of hip, speakeasy-style, upscale, and gourmet venues to offer. Coffee shops, pubs, distilleries, and rooftop bars can be found all over Philadelphia, popular with residents and out of towners alike.

☺ Go to the **Food & Drink** menu option on the **discoverphl.com** website which lists a pick of breweries and bars. Also read about the city's strict alcohol laws (◐ *Planning Your Trip, p. 112*).

◐ **Find the addresses on our maps using the numbers on the listing (e.g. ❶). The coordinates in red (e.g. C2) refer to the detachable map (inside the cover).**

OLD CITY, SOCIETY HILL & PENN'S LANDING

Old City

Local Map p. 26.

Beer Garden

⑱ Independence Beer Garden – F5 - *100 S. Independence Mall W. - ℘ (215) 922 7100 - www. phlbeergarden.com - seasonal opening times 3pm-midnight, Sat midday-2am, Sun midday-midnight - closed Mon-Tue.* Philly is a pro when it comes to beer gardens, and its most recent addition is one of the most successful. Ideally situated just a short walk from the sites of the Independence National Historical Park, this sprawling bar has various spaces to sit, mostly outside. There's a vast selection of beers, a pub menu, and lots of space to play (table football, darts, etc.), watch a game on the big screen, or even relax on a lounge chair with your toes in the sand. Ideal for a pitstop or longer pause.

Rooftop Bar

⑰ Stratus Lounge – G5 - *433 Chestnut St. - ℘ (215) 925 2889 - stratuslounge.com - closed Sun-Wed, Thu 8pm-1am, Fri-Sat 8pm-2am.* A ritzy nightspot on the 11th story of the Hotel Monaco. Enjoy views of the stars while relaxing on huge leather couches sipping excellent cocktails and snacking on tasty appetizers. A mixed clientele of locals and tourists. Lounge music and live DJs on some nights.

Ice Cream

♥ ❺ The Franklin Fountain – G5 - *116 Market St. - 11am-midnight.* A Philly institution, this quaint ice cream parlor is a go-to destination for American ice creams, sorbets, milkshakes, and other chilled treats. Adjacent to purveyor of fine candies and chocolates **Shane Confectionery** owned by the same family, the ice cream shop occupies a historic building and has its own production shop on the second floor. From the magnificent ice cream counter to the retro décor with original soda fountain, vintage cash register, and apothecary-style details, you are instantly propelled back to bygone days. The flavors range from the old classics to the more inventive with limited editions tied in with the seasons. Everything is made on the premises, and the ingredients are carefully selected, mostly organic and locally sourced. Even the packaging is fun and original. A share of sales is donated to local causes in Philly.

Fishtown

Detachable Map

On the Go/Smoothies

8 Reap Mini Mart – **G2** - *1325 Frankford Ave.* - *(724) 924 6240* - *www.reapwellness.com* - *Mon-Fri 8:30am-6pm, Sat-Sun 9am-5pm.* A cute store with a holistic approach championing healthy eating as the foundation of good self-care. All the snack, salads, and treats here are good for you and homemade, accompanied by organic drinks and vitamin or detox smoothies packed with fresh fruit and veggies. Also stocks a range of wellness products, books, and accessories.

Bar

♥ **10 Philadelphia Distilling** – **GH2** - *25 E Allen St.* - *(215) 671 0346* - *www.philadelphiadistilling. com* - *Thu 4pm-10pm, Fri 4pm-11pm, Sat 1pm-11pm, Sun 1pm-9pm - reservation only.* Established in 2005, this was the first artisanal distillery to open in Pennsylvania since Prohibition. Taking up an old brick office building, it has various industrial-styled spaces including a stunning cocktail bar with a 30-foot marble counter and traditional copper stills visible through a wall of windows. In addition to gin, the distillery makes vodka and absinth. Its flagship product is Bluecoat American Dry Gin, a premium 100% certified organic gin, five times distilled from juniper berries and citrus zest. Makes a great and affordable souvenir or gift to take home.

Kensington

Detachable Map

Coffee Shop

7 ReAnimator Coffee – **G1** - *310 Master St.* - *(267) 758 6264* - *www.reanimatorpickup.com* - *Mon-Fri 7am-3pm, Sat-Sun, 8am-3pm.* Sharing its dining area with its neighbor **Eeva** (☉ *p. 78*), this cool coffee shop is a popular hangout for local 20 somethings and the digitally connected. The coffees and teas are supplied by fairtrade roasters and plantations, while the snacks, pastries,

Philadelphia Distilling.

and treats are made using ingredients that are local and seasonal. Friendly and cheerful staff.

Northern Liberties

Detachable Map

Bar

♥ ⑨ **Yards Brewing Co.** – **G3** - *500 Spring Garden St. - ✆ (215) 525 0175 - yardsbrewing.com - Sun-Wed 11:30am-10pm, Thu-Sat 11:30-11pm.* Yards was established by Tom and Jon, two college friends who started making their own homebrews from a garage in the Manayunk district. One of the area's original microbreweries, nowadays Yards Brewing Co. is still considered a craft brewery... even if it has grown to epic proportions. A trip out to the Northern Liberties neighborhood is worth the detour: the modern brewery building is impressive, a veritable temple to beer. Yards Brewing brews over 20 beers, 11 available on tap, ranging from traditional English lagers to pale ales with subtle amber tones. There's an enormous Taproom with large communal tables, steel fermentation vats in the background, and HD TV screens, making it the ideal place to catch an Eagles game (Philly's American Football team), chat with the locals, and get the measure of the city. Food menu for lunch or dinner.

CENTER CITY & WASHINGTON SQUARE

Center City

Local Map p. 40.

Snacks/Coffee Shop

❤ **1** **High Street Philly** – **F5** - *101 S 9th St. - 🎧 (215) 625 0988 - www. highstreetonmarket.com.* The team at Fork (🎧 p. 75) is also at the helm of this cool and affordable bakery. Ideal for a breakfast or pitstop before starting your day exploring Independence National Historical Park or Washington Square. All the products are homemade using local, fairtrade products: the best breads in the country (with awards to prove it), soups, sandwiches, salads, pastas, pizzas, pastries, and other delicious morsels. The strawberry basil scone is a firm favorite.

2 **Federal Donuts** – **F5** - *21 S 12th St. - www.federaldonuts.com - several locations.* Philly's hometown hero serving fresh homemade donuts with original flavors that change with the seasons. The buffalo chicken sandwich in a brioche bun is sensational!

Bar

11 **Leda and The Swan** – **F5** - *1224 Chestnut St. - 🎧 (267) 734 1771 - www.lnsphilly.com - Wed-Thu 5pm-midnight, Fri-Sat 5pm-2am, reserve to secure seats for events - cocktails $12-18.* Stylish bar with a hip crowd. Inventive cocktails with original names, light meals, and live DJs or bands keeping you entertained.

Chinatown

Local Map p. 40.

Snacks/Coffee Shop

4 **Mayflower Café & Bakery** – **F4** - *1008 Race St. - 🎧 (215) 629 5668 - daily 7am-8:30pm.* Chinese-style bakery and tea shop popular with locals serving up savory buns, brioche rolls, coconut or mango tarts, and an assortment of coffees, teas, and bubble teas.

South Philly

Detachable Map

On the Go

Okie Dokie Donuts – **Off Map**– *1439 Snyder Ave. - 🎧 (267) 237 3786 - www.okiedokiedonuts.com - Wed-Sun 8am-3pm.* An artisanal bakery where the famous donuts are made on site, gluten free, in small batches, and in just six original flavors, including one or two vegan options. The menu changes monthly in keeping with the season, the whims of the chef running the kitchen, and the finely selected ingredients. You need to get in quick to enjoy these divine donuts—in flavors such as matcha lemon, coconut caramel, and s'mores—as they come in limited quantities and are snapped up fast by locals and foodies in the know.

Rooftop Bar

13 **Bok Bar** – **F8** - *800 Mifflin St. - 🎧 (445) 223 1607 - www.bok-bar. com - Apr-Oct - Wed-Thu 5pm-11pm, Fri-Sat 5pm-midnight, Sun 2pm-10pm.* This alternative venue in a former high school is cohabited by creatives, artists, and entrepreneurs. At the top, Bok Bar and its rooftop afford stunning panoramic views over the Philly skyline and its radiant sunsets. If you go on Friday or Saturday evening, always busy, expect a long wait in line. The young, relaxed, and unpretentious crowd go to have fun, not to be seen.

BENJAMIN FRANKLIN PARKWAY & RITTENHOUSE SQUARE

Benjamin Franklin Parkway

Local Map p. 40.

Rooftop Bar

♥ **⑮ JG SkyHigh** – **E4** - *1 N 19th St. - ℰ (215) 419 5059 - www.jgskyhigh. com - daily 7am-10pm - cocktails, wines, champagne and liquors $14-38*. Located on the 60th floor of the **Four Seasons Hotel**, this gorgeous bar, all black marble and large mirrors, offers breathtaking city views. The dining room specializes in approachable cuisine from Michelin-starred New York chef **Jean-Georges Vongerichten** (ℰ p. 82). The drinks and food menu are impeccable, and the place is a Philly highlight. Live music several times a week, a top spot for getting in the jazzy mood.

Rittenhouse Square

Local Map p. 40.

Ice Cream

③ Jeni's Splendid Ice Cream – **E5** - *1901 Chestnut St. - www.jenis. com - several locations*. Founded

by Jeni Britton in 1996, the owner is uncompromising when it comes to the provenance of the milk and the quality of the ingredients, sourced from responsible partners. The ice creams are popular for their original sometimes unexpected flavors including whisky and pecans, or seasonal varieties like eggnog.

Rooftop Bar

⑭ Wet Deck Philly – **E5** - *1439 Chestnut St. - ℰ (215) 709 8000 - www.wetdeckphilly.com - cocktails and snacks $12-25*. An oasis on the 7th story of the super hip **W Philadelphia** (ℰ p. 103), the bar overlooks the pool and there's a gorgeous terrace up there too. Find a spot according to your mood: be the center of attention near the DJ booth or stay away from prying eyes in one of the garden lounge areas.

⑯ El Techo – **E5** - *1830 Ludlow St. - www.condesaphilly.com - Mon-Thu 4pm-11pm, Fri-Sat 4pm-midnight, Sun 11am-4pm, happy hour Mon-Sat 5pm-7pm - beers, wines, cocktails $7-15, food $15-35*. Lively atmosphere, Mexican menu for both drinks (tequila-based cocktails, mezcal) and food (tacos, quesadillas, and other classics.) A popular bar, especially at happy hour.

Shopping

With no sales tax added to purchases of clothing and footwear, Philadelphia is a shopping paradise. You'll find all the major labels, mostly in the Rittenhouse Square district, around Market St. and Broad St.

Less than 20 miles from Philadelphia, King of Prussia Mall, one of the biggest shopping centers in the country, is a magnet for retail lovers who come to snap up bargains in the outlet stores where rock-bottom prices keep competitors at bay. Collectors might prefer to scour vintage shops and antique stores in the area's pretty local boroughs.

☉ **Find the addresses on our maps using the numbers on the listing (e.g. ❶). The coordinates in red (e.g. C2) refer to the detachable map (inside the cover).**

OLD CITY, SOCIETY HILL & PENN'S LANDING

Old City

Local Map p. 26.

Shops

South Street – **DG6**. This commercial street is lined with lots of independent brands and labels, as are several streets in Old City.

Jewelers' Row – **F5**. The oldest jewelers' district in the country also boasts plenty of other stores and bustling restaurants (www.jrow.org).

⓰ Art in the Age – **G4** - 116 N. 3rd St. - ℘ (215) 922 2600 - www.artintheage. com - Tue-Thu midday-7pm, Fri-Sat midday-8pm, Sun midday-6pm - closed Mon. This store has developed a line of four handcrafted liquors, including a delicious rhubarb-based variety. While you can't shop in store (for that you need to go to a liquor store), the place throws a happy hour and block party every Thursday, from

5pm, and every first Friday of the month, from 6pm. The boutique sells handcrafted goods, cosmetics, and designer apparel.

⓯ United by Blue – **G4** - 205 Race St. - ℘ (215) 278 7746 - ℘ (267) 457 3114 - unitedbyblue. com - Mon-Fri 9am-5pm. Imagined as a meeting place for local residents, this one-of-a-kind store doubles up as an events space hosting exhibitions, workshops, and the like. It's also a cafe, perfect for a coffee break or lunch, and a clothier which sells a collection of apparel online (its T-shirts are popular) and removes a pound of trash from waterways for each product purchased.

Society Hill

Local Map p. 26.

Market

❶ Headhouse Farmers' Market – **G6** - 2nd & Lombard St. - www.thefoodtrust. org/what-we-do/farmers-markets/

headhouse - Sun 10am-2pm. One of the most popular markets in Philly where you might cross paths with some of the city's famous chefs stocking up their kitchen larders. Stalls are brimming with appealing fresh produce from local farms. Houses a few gourmet spots to feast on mouth-watering snacks and other fare, including High Street Philly (*C p. 92*) and Talula's Table (*C p. 87*).

Shop

⑩ Suplex Sneakers – G6 - *533 South St. - instagram @suplexsneakers - midday-8pm, Sun midday-5pm.* Unsurprisingly, this store sells all kinds of sneakers, along with the hottest fashion accessories from around the world, and brand-name streetwear. A destination for the fashion conscious to stay in touch with the latest trends. Stocks rare and limited collector's editions too.

Fishtown

Detachable Map

Shops

⑫ Jinxed – G2 - *1331 Frankford Ave. - ℘ (215) 800 1369 - instagram @jinxedstore - 11am-6pm.* Industrial vibes aplenty at this vintage store selling an eclectic mix of apparel, footwear, accessories, furniture, and more.

⑬ Harriett's Bookshop – H2 - *258 E Girard Ave. - ℘ (267) 241 2617 - www.oursisterbookshops.com - midday-6pm.* A beautiful bookstore devoted to African American literature, authors, and activists. Also hosts music and art events.

⑭ Philadelphia Record Exchange – **G1** - *1524 Frankford Ave. - ℘ (215) 425 4389 - instagram @philarecx - 11am-8pm.* A local institution since 1985, this store buys and sells vinyl of every genre. Record collectors, on your marks!

CENTER CITY & WASHINGTON SQUARE

Center City

Local Map p. 40.

Market

❷ Reading Terminal Market – **F4** - *Market N. 12th St. et 1136 Arch St. - readingterminalmarket.org - 8am-6pm.*– The famed historic indoor market (*C p. 42*) is home to various food counters, a farmers' market, and vendors from the local area and across Philadelphia. Fill spare room in your luggage with souvenirs such as handcrafted candles and soaps, or artisanal products like chocolates, honey, or jams made by Amish farmers.

❺ Macy's – EF5 - *1300 Market St.* The Macy's building, close to City Hall, is spectacular and colossal, like a cathedral of commerce. There's even a pipe organ in the department store's main hall where concerts are performed daily to serenade your shopping experience. Major labels have concessions here—Ralph Lauren, Calvin Klein, Levi's, Michael Kors, Tommy Hilfiger, and Nike to name a few—, so you're sure not to go home empty-handed.

95

6 **Fashion District Philadelphia** – **F5** - *901 Market St.* - ℘ *(215) 925 7162 www.fashiondistrictphiladelphia.com.* Slap bang in the heart of Center City, this shopping mall offers a selection of American and international brands alongside a handful of outlet stores with knockdown prices. A practical option for time-strapped travelers unable to make it out to Philadelphia Premium Outlets, in the city suburbs (**𝒞** *p. 97*).

17 **Antique Row** – **F6** – *Pine St., between Broad St. and 9th St.* Billed as Philly's antiques quarter, this stretch is a mix of delightful vintage, gift, and interior design stores.

Washington Square

Local Map p. 40.

Shops

♥ **9** **P's & Q's** – **F6** – *820 South St.* - ℘ *(215) 592 0888* - *www.psandqs.com* - *midday-7pm, Sun midday-6pm.* Two brothers with a love of streetwear culture launched their own unisex brand now showcased in its own beautiful store. The label's designs, exclusive to Philadelphia, are based on the city's culture and love: the bang-on-trend apparel known for its vivid graphics and vintage look pays homage to historical figures and contemporary personalities with Philly roots. They also partner up with select brands to extend their collection and regularly host music, literary, and culinary events as collabs with local entrepreneurs. A fashion-conscious label with a philosophy it's hard not to love.

11 **NewsBoy Hats** – **F6** - *620 South St.* - ℘ *(610) 707 5224* - *10:30am-7pm, Sun midday-6pm.* You don't have to be a newsboy to shop here. All manner of headgear is available from hats (fedora, panama, wide-brimmed, cowboy, etc.) to caps (bearing the logos of Philly sports teams), berets, and a selection of accessories, shawls, and scarves to add that finishing touch to your look.

South Philly

Detachable Map

Market

3 **Italian Market** – **F7** - *919 S 9th St.* - *www.italianmarketphilly.org* - *10am-4pm, Sun 10am-3pm.* This market set up by the city's Italian immigrants (**𝒞** *p. 46*) is a collection of vendors' stalls and local merchants running along the sidewalk on both sides of 9th Street. The atmosphere is always buzzing and the "Italian" market is today much more international. On Sunday, vintage clothes sellers add a bustling flea market feel to the place.

Shop

7 **Molly's Books & Records** – **F7** - *1010 S 9th St.* - ℘ *(215) 923 3367* - *instagram @mollysbooksandrecords* - *10am-6pm.* Run by a married couple and their son, always cheerful and helpful! Literature-loving Molly and her music-loving husband combine their respective passions to offer a vast selection of second-hand books and vinyl.

BENJAMIN FRANKLIN PARKWAY & RITTENHOUSE SQUARE

Rittenhouse Square

Local Map p. 40.

Market

④ Rittenhouse Square Farmers' Market – **E5** – *1800 Walnut St. - www.farmtocitymarkets.com/markets/rittenhouse - Tue-Sat 10am-2pm.* Without a doubt the most popular farmers' market in Philadelphia. Local farmers come to sell their fresh, organic produce. Stop for breakfast or a savory snack at one of the bakery or homemade food stalls. In warm weather, musicians liven up the market on Saturday morning.

Queen Village

Detachable Map

Shop

❽ Philly Vintage Bazaar – **G6** – *744 S 4th St. - www.phillyvintagebazaar.com - 11am-6pm, Sun 11am-5pm.* A great destination for vintage clothes, shoes, and accessories alongside second-hand items in almost-new condition. Keep your eyes peeled for designer garments.

THE COUNTRYSIDE OF PHILADELPHIA

Map p. 66.

Shops

❶ King of Prussia Mall – *160 N Gulph Rd, King of Prussia - ✆ (610) 265 5727 -* www.simon.com/mall/king-of-prussia - 10am-9pm, Sun 11am-6pm. The region's shopping hub is one of the largest malls in the country and the largest on the East Coast. There are over 450 retailers, a mix of American and international brands, plus luxury and designer labels to boot. Ice cream shops, cafes, and places to eat (*☕ p. 88*) provide sustenance for your shopping trip.

❷ Suburban Square Ardmore – *Anderson & Coulter Ave., Ardmore - ✆ (610) 896 7560 - www.suburbansquare.com - 10am-6pm, Sun midday-6pm.* Enjoy a pleasurable shopping experience along this mall's pedestrian-friendly streets with fountains, cafes, restaurants, and terraces in the upscale borough of Ardmore. Familiar brands are tucked between thriving local boutiques. Live music and family events are programmed all year round.

Outlets

Philadelphia Premium Outlets – *18 Lightcap Rd, Pottstown - www.premiumoutlets.com/outlet/philadelphia - 10am-9pm, Sun 10am-7pm.* Featuring nearly 150 outlet stores for cost-conscious shoppers. Pick up bargains at a host of upscale American (Ralph Lauren, Nike, Gap, Michael Kors, Brooks Brothers, Under Armour) and international (UGG, H&M, etc.) merchants.

🎵 Nightlife

Vibrant, dynamic, festive, glamorous, and jazzy are just some of the words to describe Philly's art, music, and entertainment scene. Music has always been a big part of Philadelphia's soul, and the city is home to several jazz clubs whose reputation has gone national. From festivals and cultural events to live performance and gigs, there's always an excuse to explore the Philly nightlife. Here's a selection of addresses promising shared experiences, chilled vibes, or hip-swaying beats, depending on your fancy.

☛ **Find the addresses on our maps using the numbers on the listing (e.g. ①). The coordinates in red (e.g. C2) refer to the detachable map (inside the cover).**

CENTER CITY & WASHINGTON SQUARE

Center City

Local Map p. 26.

💜 **⑥ Time** – **E5** - 1315 Sansom St. - ☏ (215) 985 4800 - www.timerestaurant.net - 5pm-2am - admission $5-15 some evenings according to program. Two rooms, two ambiences. On the first floor, you can almost touch the performers in the intimate restaurant, bar, and jazz club where bands play almost nightly. With the live music filling your ears, don't expect to strike up conversation with the neighboring table! Sit back and soak up the atmosphere that heats up as the night progresses. Upstairs, the Parisian-style club hosts DJs who set the dancefloor alight every Friday and Saturday evening. It attracts a big crowd on the weekend so booking a table for dinner is recommended.

⑦ Tabu Lounge and Sports Bar – **F5** - 254 S 12th St. - ☏ (215) 964 9675 - www.tabuphilly.com - 4pm-2am, Fri-Sat midday-2am - dinner, brunch $15-35, beers and cocktails $7-15, shows and programmed performances $20. ID required at door for entry. Especially lively at happy hour, this bar is one of the most popular LGBTQ+ venues in Philly, and one of the most inclusive: everyone is welcome here, as the owners cheerfully proclaim. The atmosphere is just as festive on match days as at Sunday brunch, when drag queens run riot on stage.

Washington Square

Local Map p. 40.

② Walnut Street Theatre – **F5** - 825 Walnut St. - ☏ (215) 574 3550 - www.walnutstreettheatre.org. The oldest theater in the country (1809) puts on several musicals a year in its superb interior. Book your tickets now!

BENJAMIN FRANKLIN PARKWAY & RITTENHOUSE SQUARE

Rittenhouse Square

Local Map p. 40.

❤ ① **Kimmel Cultural Campus** – **E5** - *300 S Broad St. - Center City - ☎ (215) 790 5800 - www.kimmelculturalcampus.org - 🅿 admission fee - ♿.* This huge performing arts venue designed by the architect Rafael Viñoly (2001) is the home of a number of cultural institutions, including the outstanding Philadelphia Symphony Orchestra.

⑤ **Chris' Jazz Cafe** – **E5** - 1421 Sansom St. - *☎ (215) 568 3131 - www.chrisjazzcafe.com - Tue-Thu 4pm-midnight, Fri 4pm-2am, Sat 6pm-2am.* A Philly institution! This jazz club has hosted live jazz and blues bands and musicians for 30 years uninterrupted. Join regulars and tourists, all music loving, for dinner or a drink.

North Philadelphia

Local Map p. 40.

❤ ③ **South** – **E3** - *600 N Broad St. - ☎ (215) 600 0220 - www.southjazzkitchen.com - Thu 5pm-10pm, Fri-Sat 5pm-11pm, Sun 4pm-9pm - reservation only - dinner $30-50, ticket $10-40, check program.* A go-to destination if authentic jazz is your jam. This restaurant with a loyal clientele serves Southern American fare and welcomes live jazz, blues, and soul bands and musicians on to its stage.

Artists come from all over the country. The club stands out for its focus on promoting an eclectic bunch of local and emerging talent, from blues divas to vibraphone players.

④ **Velvet Whip** - **F4** - *319 N 11th St. - www.velvetwhipphilly.com - admission $5-15, check program.* One of the best kept secrets in Philly! This speakeasy-style basement venue doesn't have a sign out front. Look for the double doors and make your way down to the cellar. Behind the plush curtain is a club space furnished with couches and baroque velvet armchairs giving patrons full view of the stage. Jazz duos, trios, and quintets put on spectacular shows and love interacting with the audience. Purists will appreciate the venue's small capacity and cozy, glamorous vibes. A great night out.

⑧ **The Trestle Inn** – **F4** - *339 N 11th St. - ☎ (267) 239 0290 - www.thetrestleinn. com - 8pm-2am - admission $10-20 - ID required at door for entry - cocktails $12-16.* A spot popular with locals where they come to dance and party like it's the 60s and 70s. Go-go dancers (men and women) raise the temperature to the delight of patrons who shimmy and shake to the excellent Motown, disco, and funk playlist. The saying "dance like no one's watching" should be this venue's tagline!

Where to Stay

Whatever your style, you'll easily find a place to stay in the location that best suits you. Because when it comes to accommodation and hospitality, Philadelphia has it covered, so travelers are able to stick to their preferences and budget as closely as possible. From boutique hotels and bed and breakfasts to family suites and hip, upscale establishments, Philly has the right address and neighborhood for you. Note that prices fluctuate wildly based on demand, irrespective of season.

☞ Find the addresses on our maps using the numbers on the listing (e.g. ❶).
The coordinates in red (e.g. C2) refer to the detachable map (inside the cover).

OLD CITY, SOCIETY HILL & PENN'S LANDING

Fishtown

Detachable Map

100

$250-400

❤️ **⑭ Wm. Mulherin's Sons Hotel – G1** - *1355 N Front St. - ☎ (215) 291 1355 - www.wmmulherinssons. com/hotel - ✗ - 4 rooms $245-375.* There's no sign for this under-the-radar hotel. Simply present yourself at the eponymous restaurant to be shown to your room. There's just four rooms, all meticulously restored with a mix of beautiful interior design, industrial fixtures, and period details. Exposed brickwork, gleaming floorboards, bespoke wallpaper, collector's pieces, and vintage touches, you'll feel as if you've stepped into a lifestyle magazine and instantly want to move in permanently! Note that the historic elevated train occasionally passes by some windows, thankfully soundproofed. This is also part of Fishtown's charm. Style at its most singular.

⑬ Lokal Hotel Fishtown – G1 - *1421 N Front St. - ☎ (215) 291 1355 - www.staylokal.com/hotels/ fishtown-boutique-hotel/- 6 rooms $258-330.* Committed to promoting the local community, the management commissioned thirty or so local makers and craftspeople to design, fit out, and decorate the studios and apartments of this boutique hotel. In a mid-century style, the spaces are at once on trend, elegant, and minimalist. The rooms all come in different sizes. Guests share a small communal patio. The hotel has self check-in and guests are provided with a 4 digit code to their room by email. Communicate with the hotel staff via the mobile app or WhatsApp. If traveling with family or friends, you have the option to book all six rooms and hire out the entire hotel. Note: As with its neighbor, the elevated train hums by certain rooms, fitted with double-glazing (indicated as "Train Side" on the booking site to notify light sleepers).

CENTER CITY

Local Map p. 40.

$200-400

④ **The Notary Hotel, Autograph Collection** – **EF5** - *21 N Juniper St. - ☏ (215) 496 3200 - www. thenotaryhotel.com -* 🅿 ✕ - *499 rooms $220-360* ☕. Set in the old City Hall Annex dating from 1926, this hotel is a fusion of history and luxury. The original marble floors and brass moldings beautifully mingle with the contemporary decor. Well situated close to the Liberty Bell Center, the establishment has comfortable rooms with all mod cons. It also has its own Spanish-inspired restaurant, Sabroso+ Sorbo, to enjoy tapas and sangria, and a gym.

$250-600

⑤ **Loews Philadelphia Hotel**– **F5** - *1200 Market St. - ☏ (215) 627 1200 - www.loewshotels.com/ philadelphiahotel -* 🅿 ♿ ✕ - *581 rooms $269-569* ☕. In the heart of Center City and moments from City Hall, this hotel has taken up residency in America's first skyscraper. The 1930s liner-style building was originally destined to be a bank, evident from some well-preserved features, like the safe doors and Cartier chandeliers in the lobby. The rooms, all renovated in 2018, are modern and minimalist, combining style and premium comfort. At the excellent Bank & Bourbon (eatery serving modern American fare), whisky and bourbon aficionados will be in seventh heaven, guided by an expert sommelier.

Midtown Village

Local Map p. 40.

$100-450

③ **Sonder at The Arco** – **F5** - *1234 Locust St. - ☏ (617) 300 0956 - www.sonder.com - 24 rooms and suites - $109-450.* This boutique hotel takes up a historic colonial-style edifice in the heart of Midtown Village and Gayborhood. The rooms and family-friendly suites with floorboards and Philadelphian-inspired decor are comfortable. Check in using codes to the building and your room, emailed prior to your arrival. Download the easy-to-use mobile app to enjoy a digital concierge and access to a mine of information on local events during your stay dates. There's no on-site dining but the hotel has a guest lounge with sofa, fireplace, and microwave.

$250-650

♥ ② **The Guild House** – **E5** - *1307 Locust St. - ☏ (855) 484 5333 - www. guildhousehotel.com - 12 rooms and suites - $249-649 (based on whether room or suite).* This boutique hotel, set in a historic building, a gorgeous Victorian residence from 1882, was once home to a community of women activists: abolitionists, suffragettes, and artists. Each room has been decorated in honor of these visionary women. The decor is upscale with plush sofas, club armchairs, solid mahogany furniture, typewriters, and period photos with a good dose of modern design. The atmosphere is intimate and cozy and the service is discreet (you almost wouldn't know the staff were there). All dealings are done by email, down to receiving the PIN code to enter the hotel. Its central location makes it ideal for exploring historic and hip Philadelphia, in close proximity to a great many restaurants, coffee shops, and concert venues.

BENJAMIN FRANKLIN PARKWAY & RITTENHOUSE SQUARE

Benjamin Franklin Parkway

Local Map p. 40.

$350-700

6 Four Seasons Hotel Philadelphia at Comcast Center – **E4** - *1 N 19th St. - ☏ (215) 419 5000 - www. fourseasons. com/philadelphia* - 🛋 🚭 ✕ - 219 rooms $369-670 🖵. Nested at the top of the Comcast Technology Center, the tallest skyscraper in Philadelphia, this luxury establishment is a haven of peace, devoted to total rest and relaxation, affording superb city views. The sublime lobby welcomes guests up on the 60th floor. The rooms are spacious, sophisticated, and simple in their elegance, the level of comfort wholly in tune with the hotel's prestigious standing. The staff are attentive but never intrusive.

Gym, spa, and pool on the 57th floor. Several restaurants under acclaimed chefs (❻ p. 82). The panoramic bar is one of our top picks (❻ p. 93).

Rittenhouse Square

Local Map p. 40.

$250-350

1 Hyatt Centric Hotel – **E5** - *1620 Chancellor St. - ☏ (215) 985 1234 - www.hyatt.com - ✕ - 332 rooms - $239-289 🖵.* Not a complete shock, this hotel is very central, and located in Philadelphia's swankiest neighborhood. Perfect for exploring the city, pottering around the boutiques, dining at top restaurants, or catching a show. Recently opened, it has large, functional rooms. Those on the upper stories with floor to

Jason Varney/The Guild House

A room in The Guild House.

ceiling windows afford unobstructed views of Philly. The communal spaces feature industrial materials such as exposed concrete and blackened steel. Gym goers are catered for.

$150-450

**8 Sonesta Rittenhouse Square –
E5** - *1800 Market St. - ℘ (215) 561 7500 - www.sonesta.com/sonesta-hotels-resorts/pa/philadelphia/sonesta-philadelphia-rittenhouse-square - ✕ ⊥ - 439 rooms and suites - $170-410 ⊡.* A short walk from Rittenhouse Square, this modern and comfortable hotel features functional and well-appointed rooms. After a full day of sightseeing, unwind in the pool, open from May to September. Steakhouse restaurant. The hotel is known for showing in its communal areas works by local artists.

❤ **9 Element Philadelphia Downtown – E5** - *1441 Chestnut St. - ℘ (215) 709 9000 - www.marriott.com/en-us/hotels/phlel-element-philadelphia - ✕ - 460 rooms, studios and suites - $160-390 ⊡.* One of the latest additions in the heart of Philly. Ideal for families, similar to a European aparthotel, featuring spacious rooms, studios, and suites, all with fully equipped kitchens. Peaceful atmosphere with Scandi decor and greenery. The hotel is eco-conscious and partakes in various green initiatives: snacks sourced from urban hydroponic farming, paper and plastic recycled, bikes available for guest use.

$200-700

❤ **7 W Philadelphia – E5** - *1439 Chestnut St. - ℘ (215) 709 8000 - www.marriott.com/en-us/hotels/phlwh-w-philadelphia - ✕ - 295 rooms and suites - $195-680 ⊡.* One street away from City Hall, this hotel, opened in 2021, puts the focus squarely on contemporary design. Inside a 51-story tower, its modern and comfortable rooms feature floor-to-ceiling windows offering superb views of downtown. The pool on the terrace is coupled with a garden where the rooftop attracts the beautiful crowd (*ℂ p. 93*). On the lobby wall, a stunning mural pays tribute to Philly's urban identity and, all around the establishment, paintings and other artworks from local talents are on display. Cafe, restaurant, and gorgeous lobby bar, with live DJ or lounge music several times a week. The inquisitive-minded may want to take a peek behind a door off the bar leading to a private room dedicated to Grace Kelly, Philadelphia's beauty icon.

103

University City

Local Map p. 40 and Detachable Map

$200-400

❤ **10 Akwaaba B & B – B4** - *3709 Baring St. - ℘ (866) 466 3855 - www.akwaaba.com/akwaaba-philadelphia - 6 rooms $225-375.* Just minutes from Drexel University and University of Pennsylvania, this bed and breakfast will reel you in at first sight. Will it be the cachet of this magnificent 1880s manor, the gracious porch, or the friendly hospitality that will charm you the most? We'd wager it will be all three! The large dining room with a fireplace where breakfast is served and the music and reading room all contribute to the "at home" feel of the place. Each room has an en suite bathroom, and the decor is inspired by a celebrity, singer, or musician that has left an impression on Philly's history, including Patti LaBelle and Teddy Pendergrass. The house is encircled by a garden where you'll find outdoor furniture and a barbecue. A perfect destination for travelers happy to share the space and immerse themselves in the American lifestyle.

11 **Cornerstone B & B** – **C4** - *3300 Baring St. - ℘ (215) 387 6065 - www.cornerstonebandb.com - 4 rooms/2 suites - $209-329.* Located on the corner of a residential street, this picturesque Victorian house always draws the eye of passers-by. The entrance hall opens on to a grand staircase leading to the upstairs rooms and dining room where afternoon tea and breakfast are served, all made from ingredients sourced from local producers. The decor of pretty stained glass windows, patterned wallpapers, velvet drapes, and fine china takes you back to the Victorian age. The rooms and suites are beautifully elegant. There's a garden with a few outdoor tables. The couple who run the B&B go out of their way to make guests comfortable.

12 **The Study at University City** – **C5** - *20 S 33rd St. - ℘ (215) 387 1400 - www.thestudyatuniversitycity. com - ✕ - 212 rooms - $239-399* 🖫. Close to the district's two colleges, this contemporary-styled hotel is inspired by the student environment it sits within. Entering the lobby, travelers are met with large bookcases, desks, computers for guest use, pencils, pens, and complimentary postcards. Glass-topped counters exhibit items and artefacts from university collections. The comfy armchairs are an invitation to sit and read. The restaurant is popular with families coming to move their children on to campus. The rooms are modern and functional. A bunch of eateries, cafes, and shops are a short walk away.

THE COUNTRYSIDE OF PHILADELPHIA

Map p. 66.

$150-350

1 **Hotel Warner** – *120 N High St. - West Chester - ℘ (610) 692 6920 - www.hotelwarner.com -* 🅿 🏊 ♿ *- $169-330* 🖫. Accommodation is limited in downtown West Chester so the Warner Hotel is practically your only option. This small, if a little dated, hotel is right in the center, just a stone's throw from the bustling commercial and historic streets. It occupies an old 1930s movie theatre, the Warner, of which a number of Art Deco features, including the frontage, have survived. The rooms are spacious, although the decor is a tad passé. Pleasant and cheerful staff.

$200-450

♥ **2** **Inn at Whitewing Farm** –
370 Valley Rd - West Chester - ✆ (610) 388 2013 - www.innatwhitewingfarm. com - ⚂ ✕ - 11 rooms and suites - $199-429⌨. On a country lane moments from Longwood Gardens, this 18th-century gem is a secluded refuge. The impeccably tended estate lush with trees and vivid flowers has a small lake, weeping willows, and rolling hills. The charming owners welcome you into the main house where they serve afternoon tea, a gourmet breakfast, and dinner in the lounge with fireplace. The rooms and suites are in cottages and small houses dotted around the estate. They differ in size, amenities, and colorways, but they are all decorated with the same taste and elegance. Guests also have use of a lovely pool, tennis courts, wine cellar, and everything you need to prepare a delicious picnic in the bucolic surroundings. An ideal spot for a charming stay just 50 minutes from Philadelphia.

$100-200

3 **Normandy Farm Hotel & Conference Center** –
1401 Morris Rd - Blue Bell - ✆ (215) 616 8500 - www. normandyfarm.com - ⚂ ✕ - 139 rooms and suites. A historic 200-year-old estate, the old farm that houses a tavern and B&B has been transformed into a modern hotel in a rustic-chic style. The main building houses 26 suites, the restaurant, the patio, the indoor pool, and the reception rooms catering to business conferences and weddings during the sunny months. The other rooms and suites, comfortable and spacious, are set in American barn-style buildings and cottages. A 30-minute drive from the Warthon Esherick Museum and Valley Forge NHP.

$200-300

4 **Element Valley Forge** –
110 Goddard Blvd - King of Prussia - ✆ (610) 873 7200 - www. marriott.com/en-us/hotels/phlev-element-valley-forge - 🅿 ⚂ ✕ - 120 rooms - $205-305. Neighboring the King of Prussia mall and minutes by car from the entrance to the Valley Forge National Historical Park, this aparthotel-style hotel is modern and comfortable. All rooms, studios, and suites have a fully equipped kitchen. The buffet breakfast is included. The Element brand is eco-conscious, offering bike hire to guests and recycling all its paper and plastic. There's an indoor pool, plus a laundry with self-serve washers and driers, practical for roadtrippers.

PLANNING YOUR TRIP

107

Ben Franklin Bridge.
K. Huff/PHLCVB

Know Before You Go

Entry Requirements

COVID-19

🙂 Because the impact of the pandemic is ongoing, conditions of entry into the country and requirements may change without notice. Before planning your trip, always check the latest travel advice applicable for the country you are traveling from:

Australia - www.smartraveller.gov.au
Canada- https://travel.gc.ca
Ireland - www.dfa.ie/travel/travel-advice

New Zealand - www.safetravel.govt.nz
United Kingdom - www.gov.uk/foreign-travel-advice

ID – To enter the U.S. without a visa, you need to have a valid **biometric** passport. If you don't have one, a visa is required. If you're unsure, check the U.S. Embassy website:

https://au.usembassy.gov
https://ca.usembassy.gov
https://ie.usembassy.gov
https://nz.usembassy.gov
https://uk.usembassy.gov

Children, anyone under the age of 18 including babies and infants, must have their own passport to enter the U.S.: the American authorities do not accept children traveling on their parents' passport.

Visas – You do not require a visa if you are a citizen of a country in the Visa Waiver Program (VWP) and are visiting for business or leisure for **less** than **three months**. You do need a visa if you are not eligible for the VWP or are planning to work or study.

ESTA (Electronic System for Travel Authorization) – If you are a national of a VWP country, you need to register for a **travel authorization (ESTA)** three days before you travel. It costs $21 to register (online) and an approved authorization is valid for two years (**esta.cbp.dhs.gov**).

Customs – It is illegal to enter the U.S. with weapons, drugs, and certain foods, plants, and medications. The following are authorized: 1 l of alcohol (for travelers aged 21 and over), 200 cigarettes, 50 cigars, or 2 kg of tobacco. Gifts worth up to $100 can be brought in tax free (keep your receipts).

Other documentation required – An **onward/return air or sea** ticket and an **address** during your stay (can be a hotel). Electronic devices must be charged.

Traveling to Philadelphia

To find out more about the **airports** see "Getting to Philadelphia" (*p. 3*).

Airlines

🙂 Toronto (Air Canada, American Airlines), Montreal (American Airlines), London Heathrow (British Airways, American Airlines) and Dublin

(American Airlines) operate direct flights to Philadelphia.

American Airlines – www.aa.com
Air Canada – www.aircanada.com
British Airways – www.britishairways.com

Flight Comparison Sites

E-Dreams – www.edreams.com
Easy Vols – www.easyvols.com
Expedia – www.expedia.com
Skyscanner - www.skyscanner.net
Google Flight - www.google.com/flights

Money

The **U.S. dollar** ($) is divided into 100 **cents**. Notes are in denominations of $1, 5, 10, 50 and 100; coins come in 1, 5, 10, 25, and 50 cent pieces. A *dime* is a 10-cent coin, a *quarter* a 25-cent coin.

Exchange Rate (January 2023): 1 USD = 1.33 Canadian Dollar; = 0.81 British Pound; = 1.43 Australian Dollar; = 0.92 Euro; = 1.56 New Zealand Dollar.

Credit Cards –Accepted with no payment limit. The exchange rate is determined based on the day of transaction, to which commission is then added.

ATMs – ATMs are common. They apply the exchange rate at the time of the withdrawal plus a flat fee. It's more cost effective to withdraw a large amount.

☺ European bank cards can be problematic, for example if you're buying gas or renting a self-service bike. The payment terminal may ask for your zip code. To get round this if you don't have a U.S. address is to enter 00000 to complete the transaction. If the problem persists at a gas station, pay directly at the counter.

Health

Health Insurance

Don't travel without health insurance. If you do need medical treatment, costs can quickly rack up. Most tour operators offer a comprehensive insurance policy. Or contact your bank as some credit cards offer protection overseas.

☺ If you need medical attention when in the U.S., call the emergency services or go to your nearest hospital. Be aware that the cost of a visit to the emergency room can be exorbitant. If your condition isn't life threatening, find your nearest healthcare center accepting walk ins or a dedicated Walk-In Clinic, which will cost around $150 plus any treatment expenses.

Pharmacies - Medications can be purchased at drugstores and pharmacies. Most convenience stores and supermarkets sell pharmacy products.

Emergencies - Dial 911 wherever you are.

U.S. Embassies & Consulates

Australia - Embassy: Moonah Place Yarralumla - ACT 2600 Canberra - ✆ 02 6214-5600 - au.usembassy.gov. Consulates in Melbourne, Perth and Sidney.

Canada – Embassy: 490 Sussex Drive - Ottawa, Ontario K1N 1G8 - ✆ 613 238 5335 - ca.usembassy.gov. Several consulates: Calgary, Halifax, Montreal, Ottawa, Québec City, Toronto, Vancouver, and Winnipeg.

Ireland - Embassy: 42 Elgin Road, Ballsbridge - Dublin 4 ☏ 1 668-8777 - ie.usembassy.gov.

New Zealand - Embassy: 29 Fitzherbert Terrace Thorndon - Wellington 6011 - ☏ 4 462 6000 - nz.usembassy.gov. Consulate in Auckland.

United Kingdom - Embassy: 33 Nine Elms Lane , London - SW11 7US - ☏ (0)20 7499-9000 - uk.usembassy.gov. Consulates in Belfast, Edinburgh, and Hamilton.

When to Go

Philadelphia has a temperate continental climate, fairly humid, with cold winters and hot summers.

Summer - Temperatures hover around 30°C in the day and just under 20°C at night.

Winter - Cold and wet with the occasional bright, sunny day. In December-January, temperatures can be sub zero. Winters are tolerable provided there aren't snowstorms.

Spring and Fall - Generally mild, between 15 and 25°C. The weather is most pleasant for tourists in May-June. Fall is another great time to visit, when the leaves have changed color and the city is gearing up for various holidays (Halloween, Thanksgiving).

Rain - It can rain any time of year; pack an umbrella.

Weather - Check the forecasts at www.weather.gov and www.weather.com.

Further Travel Advice

Webites

Philadelphia Convention & Visitors Bureau - discoverphl.com, the most comprehensive site on Philadelphia. Packed with practical info for planning your trip divided into sections: Outdoors, Arts & Culture, Shopping, Things To Do, Food & Drink, and more. Also on Instagram: @discover_phl

Depending on where you are visiting from, you can also find information on the official travel sites of the U.S.:

www.visittheusa.com
www.visitusa.org.uk
www.visitusa.org.au

Your Stay A-Z

Dates

Dates are written with the month first: 09/07/2023 means 7 September 2023.

Eating & Drinking

You can eat any time of day in Philadelphia: a substantial breakfast from 7am followed by a light lunch eaten on the fly, and dinner, still the main meal of the day, until as late as 11pm. At the weekend, **brunch** is served from 10am to 4pm and is a popular institution in the city. In addition to street carts serving pretzels or hot dogs, fast food ($5-8) or street snacks from around the world (such as Indian or Mexican for under $20), Philly has plenty of **restaurants**, divided into three categories: international, typically American, and fine dining (over $60). Look out for Early Bird Specials or Pre-Theater Menus served early, usually from 5pm to 7-7.30pm where you can expect to eat for under 30 bucks. **Drinks** are expensive, especially wine by the glass ($8-15). Remember to add sales tax (8.875%) and the gratuity (15-20%). If you have any food left over, ask for a doggy bag to take it away.

Bring Your Own Bottle (BYOB): Alcohol licenses are so expensive that many restaurants have chosen not to sell alcoholic drinks but instead allow patrons to bring their own.

The majority of **grocery stores** have a self-serve deli section offering salads or hot food ($6-8).

⌖ *Addresses/Where* to Eat, *p. 74.*

Electricity

Only travelers from Canada won't need to bring an adaptor. European, Australian, and New Zealand electronic devices will not work without a power adaptor. You can pick one up at the airport or most supermarkets.

Embassies & Consulates

The following countries do not have a consulate in Philadelpahia. The nearest embassy for citizens of these countries is in Washington D.C.

Embassy of Australia - 1145 17th St., NW, Washington- ✆(202) 797 3000 usa.embassy.gov.au.

Embassy of Canada – 501 Pennsylvania Ave., NW, Washington- ✆ (202) 682 1740 - www.canada.ca/Canada-In-Washington.

Embassy of Ireland - 2234 Massachusetts Ave, NW, Washington - ✆ (202) 462 3939 - www.dfa.ie/irish-embassy/USA.

Embassy of New Zeland - 37 Observatory Cir., NW, Washington - ✆(202) 328 4800 - www.mfat.govt.nz.

British Embassy - 3100 Massachusetts Ave, NW Washington - ✆(202) 588 7800 -www.gov.uk/contact-consulate-washington.

Etiquette

As in most English-speaking countries,

Americans are happy to stand in line and patiently wait their turn. Most restaurants have "wait to be seated" signs. America is a friendly nation where people don't think twice about striking up a conversation with a stranger. It's probably best to avoid talking about controversial topics like religion, politics, gun laws, the death penalty, and abortion unless you're on really good terms.

Internet

Wi-Fi is available almost everywhere: hotels, coffee shops, restaurants, some public spaces, train stations, museums, airports... you get the picture.
Municipal Libraries have self-service computers and Wi-Fi available to visitors to the building.

Local Time

Philadelphia is in the Eastern Standard Time (EST) Zone.
Canada - Philadelphia is in the same time zone as Ottawa. Other Canadian provinces are 1-3 hours behind or 1 hour ahead.
United Kingdom and Ireland - 5 hours behind. When it's midday in London or Dublin, it's 7am in Philadelphia.
Australia - Philadelphia is 16 hours behind Canberra. Depending on the Australian state, deduct 14.5 or 13 hours. Midday in Canberra is 8pm the previous day in Philadelphia.
New Zealand - 18 hours behind Wellington. Midday in Wellington is 6pm the previous day in Philadelphia.
Summer time starts on the second Sunday in March and **winter time** starts on the first Sunday of November.

Mail

Postage rate: $1.40 for a postcard or letter (28 g maximum). You can buy stamps at USPS (U.S. Postal Service) branches as well as at convenience stores and drugstores. Delivery takes around 7 days to Canada, and 12 days to Europe, Australia, and New Zealand.

Opening Hours

Shops – Mon-Sat 10am-6pm, some stay open until 9pm on Thursday. Department stores are open on Sunday. Grocery stores and drugstores often open 7 days a week 10am-10pm or later.
Banks – Mon-Fri 9am-3:30pm, some open on Sat 9am-midday.
Post Offices – Mon-Fri 8:30am-5pm or 6pm, Sat morning times vary.
Museums – Generally daily 10am-5pm, often with one late-night opening weekly.

Phone

Useful Numbers

Emergencies, 911. **Information**, 411 (local number), 555 1212 (directory assistance for national use), 1-800 874 4000 ext. 324 (international number).

Local and National Calls

American phone numbers have 10 digits: the first three are the area code, followed by the seven-digit local number. For local calls (same area code), only dial the last seven digits. To call a different state (different area code), dial 1 + area code + phone number.

Calling overseas from the U.S.:
011 + country code + phone number
(without the first 0).
To Canada: 011 + 1;
To the UK: 011 + 44;
To Australia: 011 + 61;
To Ireland: 011 + 353;
To New Zealand: 011 + 64;
Calling the U.S. from overseas:
From Canada: 011 + 1;
From the UK, Ireland, New Zealand:
00 + 1;
From Australia: 0011 + 1.

Toll-Free and Special Numbers

Numbers starting with 1-800, 1-877,
1-888, 1-866, and so on are toll free
(always indicated), often used by
airlines, hotels, B&Bs, and car rental
firms. You can use them from overseas
but calls will be charged. Special
numbers are phone numbers that spell
out a word (e.g. 1800 FLOWERS) for
fast recall.

Telephone Cards – Avoid calling from
hotels, which add a tax. Instead, buy
a prepaid phone card (rates vary by
operator), available to buy at grocery
stores and newsstands. Specify if you
want to make international or national
calls. Calls are charged at low rates.
You are given a toll-free number which
you need to dial, followed by a PIN,
and then the phone number you want
to reach.

Cell Phones – To call in the States, you
need to have a tri- or quad-band cell
phone. Before you travel, contact your
operator to find out its U.S. call rates.
If you want to invest in an American
SIM card, insert it in your phone then
use prepaid cards to load it.

All operators offer SIM cards to buy,
available at grocery stores, drugstores,
newsstands, and cell phone stores.
Don't forget that you'll also be charged
for every call received.

Press

International newspapers can be found
in major cities.
Dailies – Philadelphia's two main daily
newspapers are the **Philadelphia
Inquirer** and **Philadelphia Daily News**.
The most widely read American daily is
USA Today. The **Washington Post** and
New York Times are popular too.

Public Holidays

New Year's Day: January 1.
Martin Luther King Jr.'s Birthday:
Third Monday in January.
Presidents Day: Third Monday in
February.
Memorial Day: Last Monday in May.
Independence Day: July 4.
Labor Day: First Monday in September.
**Columbus Day / Indigenous Peoples'
Day**: Second Monday in October.
Veterans Day: November 11.
Thanksgiving Day: Fourth Thursday in
November.
Christmas Day: December 25.

Safety

Downtown and tourist areas are
safe. Like in other major cities,
homelessness is widespread.
Homeless people usually go about
their business quietly and appreciate
small gestures such as giving them
cash or the rest of the meal you didn't
manage to eat at the restaurant just
before.

WE WELCOME YOU WITH OPEN ARMS

PHL

where

CURTAIN
CALL

meets

INDEPENDENCE
HALL

Discover

PHILADELPHIA

DISCOVERPHL.COM

Sightseeing

Most museums are closed on Monday and the main public holidays. Tickets are expensive, but museums usually have days with free or reduced admission.

Tourist Passes

Go City Philadelphia – *gocity.com/philadelphia/en-us*.
The All-Inclusive Pass is suitable for a short stay *(from $65/1 day, ages 3-12 $36, tiered pricing from 1 to 5 days)*. The pass gives admission to over 30 attractions, the Big Bus, and fast-tracked entry.

Guided Tours

Big Bus Hop on/off Tour – *www.bigbustours.com/en/philadelphia/philadelphia-bus-tours*. Guided tours on an open-top bus with audio commentary.
Philadelphia Sightseeing Tours Hop on/off Tour – *www.city-sightseeing.com/en/35/philadelphia*. Guided tours on an open-top bus with audio commentary.
Mural Arts Tour – *www.muralarts.org*. Self-guided and group or private guided tours of the "World Mural Capital" (*C p. 44*).
Constitutional Walking Tour – *www.theconstitutional.com*. Tours of Independence National Historical Park.

Philadelphia by Segway

Guided tours by theme (Mural Tour, Cheesesteak Tour, and others) riding a Segway *(www.phillybysegway.com)*.

Smoking

Smoking is prohibited on public transport and in public places, restaurants, and bars. You can purchase cigarettes at drugstores, grocery stores, and newsstands.

Taxes

Prices are always shown before tax (including in this guide). Taxes and gratuity inflate the check by 25-30%. The sales tax at hotels is 8.5%. In restaurants and for other services (bike rental, etc.), it's 6-8%.
☺ There's no sales tax on clothing or footwear in Pennsylvania. Philadelphia is truly a shopping paradise.

Tipping

Unless service is included (seldom the case), tip 15-20% of the check. When the tip is included, the amount is labeled as "gratuity".
At your hotel, it's customary to tip the bellstaff/porters a couple of bucks per bag and housekeeping staff $1-5 per day.

Toilets

Public toilets are few and far between. There are toilets at the Philadelphia Visitor Center Corporation if you are visiting Independence Historical Park.

Tourist Information

Philadelphia Convention & Visitors Bureau (PCVB) – *1601 Market St., Suite 200 - www.discoverphl.com*. The website is a mine of information on city events, tourist sites, things to do, practical advice, and more.

Philadelphia Visitor Center Corporation – *599 Market St. - 1 N. Independence Mall W. - ✆ 1 800 537 7676 - www.phlvisitorcenter. com.* Provides full information on Independence National Historical Park and all the sites.

Transport

⌖ *Getting to Philadelphia, p. 3.*
SEPTA (Southeastern Pennsylvania Transportation Authority) is the company that operates the region's bus, subway, and train services *(www. septa.org - see the Transport Map on the reverse side of the Detachable Map).*

Tickets

SEPTA Key – A reloadable smart card that you can use on all modes of transport: bus, subway, trolley, train.
One Day Anywhere FleX Pass – This pass can be used for up to 10 rides in a day on SEPTA buses, trolleys, subways, and trains to any regional station. *Single Pass $13/1 day, Family Pass for 5 pers. $30 - www5.septa.org/travel/ fares.*

Buses

The whole of downtown Philly and the suburbs are well served by an extensive network of bus routes. The **PHLASH** bus makes a loop around the main tourist sites in Philadelphia. *$2 per pers. or $5 for a day pass.* The service is seasonal, so check beforehand at *ridephillyphlash. com.* Info also available at *www. discoverphl.com/plan-your-trip/ philly-phlash-downtown-loop.*

Car

There's no point driving in Philadelphia, although you may want to rent a vehicle to head out to Brandywine Valley and Valley Forge, or to go on a shopping spree at the King of Prussia Mall.

Driver's License

You'll need a national driver's license older than a year to drive. An international driver's license may be required by certain rental firms.

Car Rental

Drivers must be 21 and over, and rental companies will ask for a credit card (e.g. Visa or Mastercard) as a security deposit.
Book online as soon as you can to compare prices and snag the best deal. Rental brokers often have the lowest prices: **www.rentalcars.com, www. carrentals.com, www.ebookers.com, www.expedia.com, www.kayak.com.** Most packages now include **unlimited mileage**.
Check the **insurance** policy carefully. Coverage offered by basic third-party insurance (**Liability Insurance** or **LI**), generally minimal, should be supplemented by additional protection: **SLI** (Supplemental Liability Insurance) or **LIS** (Liability Insurance Supplement), or **EP** (Extended Protection). You can sign up to different types of protection, Collision Damage Waiver, **CDW**, or Loss Damage Waiver, **LDW**, which covers the cost of repairs in the event of an accident or theft, insurance that is automatically included if you pay with a Mastercard Gold or Visa Premier card.

Cycling

The city is flat and boasts almost 200 miles of cycle lanes, making it an ideal city to explore on two wheels (*see Philly by Bike, p. 14*).

Indego – Philadelphia has its own public bicycle sharing system, **Indego**, with over 130 stations. Pay by credit card (*$15 for 24 hour access, unlimited usage for the first 60 minutes then 20 ¢/min. For electric bikes, 20 ¢/min. from the first minute of use - www.rideindego.com*).

Other Rental Sites: *www.phillybiketours.com* and *wheelfunrentals.com/pa/philadelphia/boathouse-row*.

Subway

The city has **subway and Trolley** systems that you may not even need to use much if at all, given that Philadelphia is a very walkable city (except for traveling from the airport or train station). The two subway lines are **Market-Frankford Line** (blue on the map) and **Broad Street Line** (orange). The **Trolley** lines are green.

Taxis

Taxis are plentiful: you can hail one anywhere in Center City. Two main companies operate: Yellow Cab and Philadelphia Taxi Cab (cream and green cars).

Train

SEPTA regional trains serve a number of towns and destinations outside the city such as the airport, Germantown, and Wilmington.

Uber

The most efficient way to get around Philadelphia, especially after a long day of sightseeing.

Walking

Philadelphia is hailed as one of the best pedestrian cities in the U.S. It's easy to find your bearings in the city and get around thanks to the grid plan designed by Philly's founder William Penn and which extends for 25 blocks between the Schuylkill River and the Delaware River. City Hall's tower makes a practical reference point.

Road Rules

The **speed limit** is 70 miles per hour on most interstate highways when indicated. In the absence of signs, the speed limit is generally 55 or 65 mph on highways and expressways, 25-35 mph in residential areas, and 15mph in school zones (even one mile over the speed limit could get you in trouble). Drivers are prohibited from overtaking a school bus if its lights are flashing.

Gas

Gas prices in the U.S. are the lowest among economically advanced countries. Gas is sold by **gallon** (3.8 l). Except for large vehicles, use **regular unleaded**. Many gas stations accept card payments and self-serve pumps operate 24/7.

Festivals and Events

Highlights by Month

January
▶**Mummers Parade** – *Jan 1.* One of the oldest parades in the country: the Mummers, sporting elaborate costumes, "strut" from City Hall to Washington Ave via Broad St. (☞ *p. 46*).

March
▶**Philadelphia Flower Show** – *Early March.* The biggest horitcultural event in the country and the world's first (running since 1829).

▶**St Patrick's Day** – *March 17.* A celebration of Ireland and all things Irish. A lively day in Philly, which is home to a large Irish community, with parades, gigs, and parties in pubs.

April
▶**Shofuso Cherry Blossom Festival** – A festival devoted to Japanese art, music, and food during cherry blossom season, culminating at the Horticulture Center in Fairmount Park.

May
▶**Italian Market Festival** – *Third weekend in May.* The Italian Market on 9th St. (☞ *p. 46)* is the setting for a traditional festival featuring a procession of saint statues and lots of Italian delicacies to sample.

May-June
▶**Philly Beer Week** – *Late May-early June.* One of the biggest festivals of its kind in America and a chance to try a host of locally produced beers. *phillylovesbeer.org.*

▶**Fete Day** – *First Sat in June.* Residents of Elfreth's Alley open the doors to allow visitors a glimpse of their 18th- and 19th-century homes. Costumed historic reenactments.

▶**Philly Gay Pride Month** – *June 1 to 30.* Philadelphia's LGBTQ+ community is one of the largest in the country. Parades, workshops, and other events are programmed all through June.

▶**Manayunk Arts Festival** – *Last weekend of June.* The hip district of Manayunk, with its cool lofts and Victorian houses, hosts an annual art festival where over 300 artists come and show their works.

June-July
▶**Wawa Welcome America Festival** – *June 19-July 4.* Celebrate America's national day with shows, parades, fireworks and more sponsored by Wawa convenience stores. *welcomeamerica.com.*

September-October
▶**Fringe Festival** – Over a thousand experimental performances take over all parts of the city with theater, dance, visual arts, and more.

▶**Halloween Nights at the Eastern State Penitentiary** – *Late Sep-early Nov.* The oldest penitentiary opens its cells for a spooky immersive experience (☞ *p. 56*).

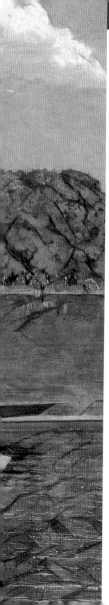

FIND OUT MORE

The Biglin Brothers Racing (1872) by Thomas Eakins.
Gibon Art/Alamy/hemis.fr

Key Dates

1607 – Foundation of Jamestown, on the coast of Virginia, the first English settlement in the New World.
1626 – Peter Minuit purchases the island of Manhattan from Native Americans.
1644 – Birth of William Penn.
1668-1669 – William Penn is imprisoned in the Tower of London for his religious convictions.
1681 – King Charles II of England grants William Penn a large area of land west of New Jersey.
1682 – William Penn founds Philadelphia. Penn signs a peace treaty with the Lenape.
1683 – German immigrants settle in the area today known as Germantown.
1700 – Philadelphia and New York tie to become the second-most populated cities in the U.S. after Boston.
1723 – Benjamin Franklin finds work as a printer in Philadelphia.
1756 – Start of the Seven Years' War.
1763 – The Treaty of Paris ends the Seven Years' War. France loses Canada and its land east of the Mississippi to Britain and Florida to the Spanish.
1764-1767 – The British impose taxes on the American colonists.
1773 – When Britain refuses to ban the tax on tea, American protesters dump chests of tea into Boston harbor (*Boston Tea Party*).
1775 – Start of the American War of Independence.
1776 – The Declaration of Independence is signed on July 4, in Philadelphia.

1780 – Home to 45,000 citizens, Philadelphia is the most populated city of the Thirteen Colonies.
1781 – The Siege of Yorktown (Virginia): the British troops surrender.
1783 – The Treaty of Versailles ends the American War of Independence.
1790 – Philadelphia becomes the temporary capital of the U.S. for 10 years while Washington is being built.
1803 – American congress ratifies the purchase of Louisiana from France.
1812 – Start of the War of 1812 with Britain. The war affected the maritime trade of Philadelphia, which was dethroned by New York.
1861 – The American Civil War breaks out.
1863 – The Battle of Gettysburg is a victory for the Union forces. Slaves are freed by the Emancipation Proclamation issued by President Lincoln.
1865 – End of the American Civil War. Congress votes to abolish slavery. President Abraham Lincoln is assassinated. Philadelphia becomes the center of the American industrial revolution, drawing thousands of African American migrants.
1870 – Ratification of the Fifteenth Amendment prohibiting any denial of a citizen's right to vote.
1876 – Philadelphia hosts the first World's Fair on American soil.
1917 – The U.S. enters World War I.
1920 – The Nineteenth Amendment recognizes the right of women to vote.

1929 – The Wall Street Crash and the start of the Great Depression.
1933 – Roosevelt enacts the New Deal, a program of social reforms.
1941 – Japanese troops attack Pearl Harbor; the U.S. enters World War II.
1944 – The Allied Forces land in Normandy (D-Day).
1945 – End of World War II. Death of Roosevelt.
1950 – Philadelphia has a population of over 2 million.
1963 – Assassination of President Kennedy in Dallas (Texas). The police suppress protests by civil rights activists in Montgomery (Alabama).
1964 – Congress passes the Civil Rights Act. The U.S. launches its first air strikes against North Vietnam.
1965 – The Voting Rights Act prohibits racial discrimination in voting.
1968 – Martin Luther King is assassinated in Memphis (Tennessee).
1969 – Astronaut Neil Armstrong walks on the Moon.
1970 – Following the 1960s race riots in response to the civil rights movement, social problems, and unemployment, the white middle classes start to leave the city center: Philadelphia loses over 13% of its population.
1973 – The last American troops leave Vietnam.
1974 – The Watergate scandal, leading to President Nixon's resignation.
1979 – A serious nuclear incident occurs at Three Mile Island in Pennsylvania. Start of the hostage crisis in Iran and end of President Carter's term.
1981 – Ronald Reagan is elected the 40th President of the U.S.
1990 – Start of the Gulf War.

1999 – Bill Clinton is impeached.
2001 – George W. Bush becomes the 43rd President of the U.S. Terrorist attacks on the World Trade Center in New York . Bush sends troops to Afghanistan to destroy Al-Qaida's training camps.
2003 – The U.S. declares war on Iraq in violation of the UN Charter.
2004 – George W. Bush is reelected.
2005 – Hurricane Katrina devastates the Gulf of Mexico and New Orleans.
2006 – The U.S. population reaches 300 million.
2008 – The subprime mortgage crisis triggers a global financial crisis. Barack Obama is elected 44th President of the U.S.
2011 – U.S. special forces kill Osama Bin Laden in Pakistan.
2012 – Reelection of Barack Obama.
2016 – Donald Trump is elected 45th President of the U.S.
2017 – Weinstein scandal and the MeToo movement.
2020 – Joe Biden becomes the 46th President of the U.S. Start of the COVID-19 pandemic.
2021 – Pro-Trump rioters storm the U.S. Capitol.
2022 – John Fetterman wins the midterm senatorial election, flipping Pennsylvania, considered a swing state, to the Democratic camp.

Philadelphia History

Although the **Pilgrim Fathers** landed in Boston, the history of the country was also written in other major cities on the East Coast: New York, Washington, and, above all, Philadelphia.

The First Americans

The first inhabitants of the Americas arrived around 28,000 years ago by crossing the Bering Strait when it wasn't submerged by water. At the time when Christopher Columbus discovered the New World, between 1.5 and 2 million people were living on the American continent.

When European colonization began, the **Eastern Woodlands** people inhabited a vast forested area, bordered south by the Atlantic coast and the Gulf of Mexico, west by the Appalachian Mountains and the Mississippi Valley, and north by the Great Lakes region. They practiced hunting and gathering, fishing and farming, sourcing food and building materials from the dense Eastern Woodlands region. Divided into two linguistic groups—the **Algonquians** and the **Iroquois**—, the Eastern Woodlands people were organized in tribes. The northeast was home to the Massachusett, Pequot, Mohawk, Oneida, and **Delaware** tribes; the Midwest and Great Lakes region, the Shawnee, Illinois, Sauk, Ottawa, Fox, and Potawatomi.

The First Colonies

Spanish, Dutch, French, and British adventurers were the first to explore the New World. Spain, the most powerful European nation at that time, claimed Florida, the Gulf of Mexico, and California; Britain was interested in the East Coast, while the French settled in Canada and along the Mississippi. In 1565, the Spanish founded the first permanent colony in **St. Augustine** (now Florida). In 1585, the English established their first settlement in Roanoke. Then, in 1607, they founded **Jamestown** in Virginia. By 1624, the town was a prosperous colony thanks to abundant tobacco crops. Over 600 miles north, the Puritans, strict Calvinists from England, had, in 1620, established the colony of **Plymouth** and, from 1629, colonized the entire Boston region.

In 1660, the return of Charles II to the English throne set a new wave of colonization in motion. A royal charter defined the boundaries of Connecticut in 1662 and of Carolina in 1663. In 1664, the city of New York—colonized by the Dutch under the name New Amsterdam in 1624 —was claimed by the British. **Pennsylvania** and Delaware followed suit.

Once Upon a Time in Pennsylvania

From the mid-17th century, Swedish, British, and Dutch immigrants settled along the banks of the Delaware.

The struggle for the control of the Delaware Valley was a victory for the British. In 1681, **William Penn**, the son of the English admiral Sir William Penn, began his "crusade" in the New World. The educated and wealthy young Penn, who converted to Quakerism, a radical Puritan sect, was imprisoned in the Tower of London for his religious beliefs. Fleeing religious persecution in England, he founded a pacifist Quaker colony in America on a vast area of land granted by King Charles II as payment for a debt. Penn established his colony on a strip of land bound by the **Delaware River** and the **Schuylkill River**, purchased from the **Lenape**. There he founded **Philadelphia in 1682**, a name meaning the **City of Brotherly Love** in Greek, where he strongly promoted religious tolerance and liberal government. The city was situated in the heart of a wooded region he named after his father: Pennsylvania ("Penn's woodlands"). Penn planned the city in a rectangular grid pattern that was used as a model across the country. For the first time, streets were numbered and Philadelphia was the first city to use an alphanumeric address naming system. The prosperous colony attracted Quakers and European immigrants seeking religious freedom and tolerance. By 1700, it was, second to Boston, the most populated colony, the country's main economic center, and one of its largest ports.

Colonial Life

Between 1700 and 1775, in the wake of waves of German, Dutch, Irish, and Scottish immigrants coming over in search of a better life, the population grew almost tenfold. In 1700, 250,000 colonists inhabited the continent; by 1800, they numbered 5.3 million.

New York, Boston, Philadelphia, and Charleston flourished. Although it was less populated than major European cities—by the mid-18th century, Philadelphia counted 25,000 residents compared with London's half a million—, these thriving cities were not just important economic hubs but lively centers of culture too. While the **economy** in the North was driven by trade and in the South by agriculture (cotton, tobacco, and rice), American culture was taking shape. Before the American War of Independence, the country already had seven **universities,** including Harvard, Yale, Princeton, Brown, and **Penn** (University of Pennsylvania), founded in 1740. This conference of universities was dubbed the **Ivy League**, with Philadelphia regarded as the cultural hub of the New World and nicknamed the "Athens of America".

The Crucible of Independence

In the late 18th century, desire for independence grew among many colonists who were increasingly critical of the British government. The introduction of new taxes, and above all a tax on tea, was the straw that broke the camel's back. In December 1773, a group of patriots boarded ships in Boston Harbor and chucked all their cargo of tea chests into the water.

125

The protest, which became known as the **Boston Tea Party**, prompted the British to take a tougher stance on the rebellious colonists. Due to Philadelphia's dense population and prosperity, it was the natural location for the first **Continental Congress** (1774), convened to discuss the strained relations between the Old World and the New World. The colonists met in Philadelphia, in what is today called **Independence Hall**, in July 1776, and adopted the **Declaration of Independence**, officially breaking ties with Britain. Written by **Thomas Jefferson**, the Declaration was inspired by the spirit of Enlightenment and the notion that a nation's government has a social contract with its people. During the first months of the American War of Independence, Britain had the upper hand. Then in December 1776, General **George Washington**'s victory over British General William Howe, in Trenton, changed the course of the conflict. In 1778, the colonial cause gained new support when France sided with the colonial army. In 1781, the French and American armies trapped General Charles Cornwallis and his troops on the **Yorktown** peninsula.

Cut off from the British navy and under threat from the French fleet, Cornwallis surrendered.

The **Treaty of Versailles,** signed in 1783, marked the end of the war: the young nation—its borders stretching from the East Coast to the Mississippi—had won its independence.

During the 1790s, Philadelphia temporarily served as the capital of the United States until the government headquarters were transferred to Washington in 1800. Philadelphia's economic prosperity was driven by the industrial revolution which attracted waves of immigrants to the city.

The Question of Slavery

By 1850, Americans had a proud **sense of national identity**: the population numbered 23 million, industrial production was at its highest levels, and the literary rate exceeded that of Europe. Yet this optimism was overshadowed by the dark cloud of slavery, an institution that had driven a deep wedge between the North and the South. In 1860, the slave population of the U.S. was 4 million, most of whom lived in the South. For Southerners, the abolition of slavery would bring an end to their economic model and way of life. The issue turned violent and an **abolitionist movement** was organized. The abolitionists set up the **Underground Railroad**, a clandestine network of people helping slaves escape to the North and Canada. Many churches played an important role in the network, in particular the Quakers in Philadelphia. A leading abolitionist was **William Still**, a freed African American living in Philadelphia, regarded as the "father of the Underground Railroad". He helped hundreds of enslaved people escape, hiding some of them in his home in Philadelphia.

Even though the Emancipation Proclamation (issued by President Abraham Lincoln in 1863) freed slaves on paper, freedom for slaves only truly came into effect at the

George Washington At Valley Forge, by Frederick Coffay Yohn.

end of the American Civil War. It was the adoption of the **Thirteenth and Fourteenth Amendments** which did the most to help the cause, abolishing slavery (1865) and securing civil rights (1868) following a war that left 620,000 soldiers dead. The **bloodiest** conflict in American history.

The Country's Sixth-Largest City

Philadelphia's development was on an upward trajectory until the end of World War II when it entered a period of severe economic decline that lasted until the late 1980s. The 1990s marked the start of a renaissance for the city and the regeneration of its downtown area. Nowadays, the economy of the

sixth-largest city in the United States is driven by the healthcare and business services sectors.

A leading center of arts and culture, Philadelphia is home to three major universities—Pennsylvania, Drexel, and Temple. It's a sports-loving city too, celebrated through local teams like the Philadelphia 76ers (basketball), Eagles (American football), Flyers (ice hockey), and Phillies (baseball).

From his privileged position atop City Hall, Philadelphia's founding father William Penn seems to contemplate his child and proclaim for all eternity, as he did in his prayer: "And thou, Philadelphia... what love, what care, what service and what travail, there have been to bring thee forth."

Architecture

American architecture and art were marked by a unique contradiction: a desire to break away from European models and the persistence, after all, of their influence. In this regard, the absence of binding standards, the vastness of the available land, and the diversity of the climates contributed to the emergence of a diverse range of styles. From this perspective, Philadelphia is one big open-air museum.

Survival Architecture

The East Coast of the United States has been indelibly shaped by waves of immigrants as much as technological advances and esthetic revolutions. When the European colonists landed in America in the 16th and 17th century, survival was their main concern, so they built their modest houses based on the traditions from the countries they left behind using the materials found on their new continent. Many Scandinavian colonists traveled south to the Delaware Valley and constructed log cabins with three rooms arranged around a central fireplace.

The Georgian Style

Developed in England during the reigns of the monarchs George I, George II, George III, and George IV by architects the likes of **Christopher Wren** and **James Gibbs**, the Georgian style became popular across the pond from the 1720s. The buildings' symmetrical façades, classical ornamentation, and sober, rather formal elegance, pleased America's new merchant class who commissioned large residencies made of wood, stone, and brick in the country's port cities. A typical **Georgian house** has a roof with two or four slopes, or a mansard roof, and a symmetrical front emphasized by rows of regular sash windows. In the center, the porch, surmounted by a semicircular or rectangular window, is often flanked by pilasters supporting an entablature.

Georgian houses open into a central hallway fitted with fireplaces. The rooms, larger than in previous styles, had specific functions (a music room or dining room, for instance) and are decorated with carved paneling, stucco, and bright colors.

Several examples of this style can be seen in Philadelphia. The brick houses that line **Elfreth's Alley** are some of the earliest examples and are classified as a National Historic Landmark. Designed by Robert Smith in 1770, **Carpenters' Hall**, a two-story red-brick building crowned by a beautiful dome and a weather vane, is lauded as the finest example of Georgian architecture in the country. It provided inspiration for many other historic buildings.

Neoclassical Styles

After the American War of Independence, the **Adam style**, a British neoclassical style inspired by Roman villas, became all the rage. Imported into the United States under the name **Federal style**, its main features were simple forms and understated elegance. Floral garlands and wreaths adorned the walls, mantelpieces and entrances, while oval and round rooms were a major innovation of the time. While the **Pine Building** at Penn Hospital (1755) combines the Federal and Colonial styles, a **Hill-Physick House** (1786), in the **Society Hill** district, is in the Federal style exclusively.

The architects of public buildings also looked to antiquity for inspiration. An admirer of ancient Greek architecture, British-born architect **Benjamin Latrobe** (1764-1820), who settled in the U.S. in 1796, built the **Bank of Pennsylvania** (1798, no longer standing) in the style of an Athenian temple. This first monument of the **Greek Revival** inspired other public edifices. The façade with its Greek temple pediment became a common feature of banks, administrative buildings, churches, and residencies, to the extent that the neoclassical style became known as the National style. In the eyes of the educated elite, it created a symbolic tie between the ancient Greek republic and the nascent American nation.

Although **John Haviland** (1792-1852) was a major proponent of the Greek Revival style, he added his own more modern touches. He oversaw the construction of some of the city's most iconic structures, most notably The **Franklin Institute** and the **Walnut Street Theatre**. In 1829, Haviland completed the **Eastern State Penitentiary**, a revolutionary prison designed with a star-shaped floor plan to keep prisoners separate, a model that was copied around the world.

Victorian Eclecticism

The start of the Victorian era in Britain introduced an eclectic range of styles, such as **Gothic Revival**—lancet windows, steep gables, and carved cornices—or the more formal **Italianate style**—square towers, low-pitched roofs, rounded windows. More elaborate still were buildings in the **Second Empire style** featuring Italianate details combined with a mansard roof or classical ornamentation.

As the epicenter of the American industrial revolution, Philadelphia had always been progressive, and the architects of the day explored traditional styles through the lens of emerging technologies. **Frank Furness** (1839-1912) was one of the highest-paid architects of the time and most representative of the Victorian era in the late 19th century. He designed over 600 buildings, including the **Pennsylvania Academy of Fine Arts** in 1871. Furness combined diverse materials—iron, terra cotta, glass—, reflecting the new industrial era. Many of his buildings were considered outdated in the 20th century and sadly torn down. One building that was almost dismantled was **City Hall**. And yet it stands as the very symbol of Philadelphia. Designed by **John McArthur Jr.** and **Thomas Ustick Walter** in the Second Empire style, the building took nearly 30 years and 25 million dollars to complete (1871-1901). Many Philadelphians were angered by its opulence. Not only had its style fallen out of fashion by the time it was finished, its claim to be the tallest building in the world was lost to the Eiffel Tower the year work was completed. There was talk of tearing down the monument in the 1950s, but it was saved by the astronomical demolition costs!

Cret's Stamp

In 1907, the French architect **Paul Philippe Cret** (1876-1945) first introduced his modern neoclassical style to Philadelphia: he removed the Greek orders but retained the classical sense of proportion, balance, and symmetry. Cret designed several of the country's most iconic buildings including the Federal Reserve, the Folger Shakespeare Library in Washington, and the incredible Cincinnati Union Terminal. His stripped-down classicism can be seen in war monuments he designed in **Valley Forge** and **Gettysburg.** An adopted Philadelphian, Cret gave the city some of its finest assets: the **Benjamin Franklin Parkway**, the exquisite **Rodin Museum**, and **Benjamin Franklin Bridge**.

The Philadelphia School

Louis Kahn (who studied under Cret) and Robert Venturi started the postmodern movement in the 1960s. Postmodernism was an attempt to resist the predominant international style.

The buildings of the "Philadelphia School" were designed to integrate into cities rather than shape them. It was also a social movement spurred by the desire to construct affordable housing such as Guild House on Spring Garden St. Designed in 1963 by Venturi, it is one of the earliest examples of postmodernist architecture. The School's leader Kahn built in Philadelphia several structures exemplifying postmodernist ideals, including the Richard Medical Research Laboratory on Penn Campus (1965) and the revolutionary Esherick House in Chestnut Hill.

The Sky's the Limit

Until the 1980s, there was an unwritten rule that no building should be taller than the statue of William Penn perched over 1,000 feet above the city on top of City Hall. This rule was broken in 1987 when **One Liberty Place**—an Art Deco interpretation of the Chrysler Building in New York—was erected by the architect **Helmut Jahn** (1940-2021). Despite the controversy it caused, it was declared "the most beautiful skyscraper in Philadelphia". It sparked the race to the sky, and in 2008 the **Comcast Center** earned the title of the tallest building in the city. This was beaten in 2018 by the **Comcast Technology Center** which, 60 stories and 1,121 feet high, became the tallest tower outside Manhattan and Chicago. Philadelphia at last had its skyline, the quintessential silhouette that every North American city strives to possess.

Philadelphia: The Cradle of American Art

Initially influenced by European art, American painting can be characterized by a quest for its own identity. America's first national artists wished to capture daily life in the country but also great men, and nature in all its majesty.

The First American Painters

Sometimes called the father of American painting, **Benjamin West** (1738-1820), a Quaker born in Philadelphia, spent the last years of his life in London after making a European tour during which he found inspiration in works by the great masters. He was the first American artist to achieve an international reputation. Several artists were trained in his London studio, most notably **Gilbert Stuart** (1755-1828), famed for his oil paintings of George Washington, and **Charles Willson Peale** (1741-1827). The latter is regarded as the first resident painter of American history and founder, in 1805, with the sculptor William Rush, of the **Pennsylvania Academy of the Fine Arts**, the first school of its kind in the U.S., which went on to form generations of American artists.

Painting America

Arriving in Philadelphia from England in 1818, **Thomas Cole** (1801-1848) sought to capture the unspoiled Hudson Valley and Catskill Mountains as a natural Eden. Widely regarded as the first American landscape painter, he founded the **Hudson River School**. This art movement brought together painters influenced by European Romanticism and the classical landscape tradition (Poussin, Lorrain, Turner), active between the years 1820 and 1880, who wanted above all to immortalize the beauty of America's landscapes. Owing to their attention to effects of light, the second generation of American landscape artists is labeled as **Luminists**. This includes **Fitz Hugh Lane** (1804-1865), a marine artist, and **Martin Johnson Heade** (1819-1904), a painter of Pennsylvanian landscapes.

Towards Impressionism

Born in Massachusetts and taught in Russia and Paris, France, where he settled in 1855, **James Abbott McNeill Whistler** (1834-1903) radically transformed American painting, eschewing bitumen, shadows, opaqueness, and thick brushstrokes in favor of light, harmonious colors, sketching, and the suggestion of form through the faintest of lines. He believed painting should capture the imagination, like music to the ear, through a gentle process of osmosis. **John Singer Sargent** (1856-1925), who also worked in Europe, is known primarily for his sublime portraits of members of high society. Born in

Philadelphia, **Mary Cassatt** (1844-1926), who spent most of her life in Paris, was strongly influenced by the **Impressionists**, the likes of Edgar Degas and Camille Pissarro, who became close friends of hers. She is regarded as one of America's leading lights of Impressionist art. She was also one of the first "women artists" to be actively engaged in feminism and the suffragette movement.

A Divide in Painting

The Post-Impressionist painters **Maurice Prendergast** (1859-1924) and **Thomas Eakins** (1844-1916), who hailed from Philadelphia, moved away from the academic bias in favor of realism. A pupil under Eakins, **Henry Ossawa Tanner** (1859-1937), the first African American artist to achieve renown outside the U.S., also moved away from the academic tradition, imbuing the paintings drawn from his experiences with a profound sense of spirituality. Eakins' oeuvre influenced that of **Robert Henri** (1865-1929), trained at the **Pennsylvania Academy of the Fine Arts** in Philadelphia, then in Paris. With a group of artists, which included **George Luks** (1867-1933), **William Glackens** (1870-1938), and **John Sloan** (1871-1951), he responded to the extreme meticulousness and frivolity of Impressionist art by painting the harsh realities of life in the impoverished neighborhoods of New York. These artists, who saw painting as akin to journalism, sought to show the most trivial details, right down to trash cans in the street, which earned

the movement the name the **Ashcan School**.

A Turning Point

On February 17, 1913, the International Exhibition of Modern Art opened in New York City, displaying around 1,600 artworks, a third of which came from outside the U.S. Known as the **Armory Show** (it started in the city's 69th Regiment Armory on Lexington Avenue), it attracted hundreds of thousands of visitors. The public, drawn by the reportedly scandalous Post-Impressionist, Fauvist, Cubist, and other art on show, featuring distorted images, provocative subjects, gaudy colors, and childish forms, were dumbfounded by the avant-garde European art exhibited. Going against the incredulous or sneering public, American collectors, the likes of, Walter Arensberg, Lillie P. Bliss, **Dr. Barnes**, and Duncan Phillips, found their calling.

Everyday Painting

Stuart Davis (1892-1964), born in Philadelphia and a pupil under Henri, was one of the youngest painters to show his work at the controversial Armory Show. Influenced by Fauvism for its colors and Cubism for its forms, he went on to be a major proponent of Cubism in America. He is nevertheless more famous for his still lifes, abstract landscapes, and depiction of everyday objects and themes, inspired by the Ashcan School. With his paintings of Lucky Strike packets (1921) and series of "egg beaters" (1927), Stuart Davis was a herald of Pop Art. A painter of the everyday similar to one of his contemporaries, **Edward Hopper** (1882-1967).

Andrew Wyeth Against the Stream

The onset of World War II brought an influx of **European artists**, such as Max Ernst, Yves Tanguy, and Salvador Dalí, to New York City. During the 1940s, this flourishing new crucible of contemporary art produced its own movement: **Abstract Expressionism**. The proponents of this radical art movement included adepts of **Action Painting**—including **Jackson Pollock** (1912-1956), its creator, **Willem De Kooning** (1904-1997), and **Franz Kline** (1910-1962)– and the representatives

of **Color Field,** like **Mark Rothko** (1903-1970) and **Barnett Newman** (1905-1970).

In parallel, the painter **Andrew Wyeth** (1917-2009), originating from Chadds Ford in the Brandywine Valley, was interested in painting the daily life and people of rural America, reacting to a society changing too rapidly with his own brand of nostalgia. He captured the American ideal, very different from Pollock's violent depictions and Warhol's consumerist Pop Art images. His painting *Christina's World* (1948) has become an iconic image of the United States, like that of another celebrated American realist painter who Wyeth admired: Edward Hopper.

photosublime/Alamy/hemis.fr/© Andrew Wyeth/Adagp, Paris 2023

Christina's World (1948) by Andrew Wyeth.

The Sound of Philadelphia

Classical Music

The **Philadelphia Orchestra** is one of the "Big Five", the best five orchestras in the U.S. along with those of New York, Boston, Chicago, and Cleveland. It was founded in 1900 and its musical direction has been in the hands of some of the world's greatest musicians: Eugène Ormandy, Riccardo Muti, and Christoph Eschenbach, to name a few. It was there that **Rachmaninoff** composed his Piano Concerto No. 4 in 1927, and his Symphony No. 3 in 1936. Today it is directed by **Yannick Nézet-Séguin** (**ⓒ** p. 17), who describes the Philadelphia Orchestra as: "One of the very few orchestras in the world nowadays which has a recognizable sound. There is a depth, a richness, and a generosity to the sound." The orchestra's home is the **Kimmel Cultural Campus** whose performance hall with extraordinary acoustics was designed by Rafael Viñoly, inspired by a cello. In summer, the orchestra takes over the **Mann Center for the Performing Arts**, in Fairmount Park, where it performs outside.

Musical Comedy

New York doesn't have the monopoly for musical theater on the East Coast. When in Philly, check out the **Broadway Series** presented by the Kimmel Center. The program is produced at the **Academy of Music**, the oldest working opera house in the country (1857). The **Walnut Street Theatre**, another historic venue (1809), puts on a whole season of musicals good enough to rival any Broadway production.

The Sound of Philadelphia

This style of soul music that emerged in Philadelphia was a big hit in the 1970s. It is characterized by jazz and funk influences and sumptuous instrumental arrangements with violins and guitars, brass, choirs, and silky-smooth vocalists. Philly soul was a precursor to disco, launched by the record label **Philadelphia International Records**. The music was embodied by artists the likes of Leon Huff, Kenny Gamble, Billy Paul, Harold Melvin & the Blue Notes, The Three Degrees, Teddy Pendergrass, **Patti LaBelle** (**ⓒ** p. 137) and many more. The success of these productions enticed performers from all over to come to **Sigma Sound Studios** in Philadelphia, such as **David Bowie** to record *Young Americans* (1974) and the **Jacksons** for *The Jacksons* (1976).

Melody Gardot, the New Philly Sound

Melody Gardot began playing the piano at the age of nine and performing in Philadelphia's piano bars at the age of 16. A guitarist too, she lists blues, jazz, folk, pop, rock, and classical music as her influences. Her references range from Billie Holiday to George Gershwin by way of Judy Garland, Miles Davis, Radiohead, and bossa nova. She released her first album *Worrisome Heart* in 2008 to immense critical and commercial acclaim.

Philadelphians Forever

John Coltrane (1926-1967)

John Coltrane is regarded as the most avant-garde musician in the history of jazz, along with Charlie Parker. He moved to Philadelphia with his family in 1943 and took music lessons at the Ornstein School of Music. At 17, he enrolled at the Granoff School of Music, in Philadelphia, to study music theory to underpin his solid practical knowledge. He played in the groups of some of the biggest names in jazz: Dizzy Gillespie and Miles Davis between 1955 and March 1961, and Thelonious Monk from 1957, recording several masterpieces with these jazz legends. Between 1955 and 1967, John Coltrane revolutionized jazz, becoming a figurehead of free jazz. Coltrane also battled with drug and alcohol addiction in these early years. In 1957, Coltrane returned to stay with his mother in Philadelphia and went to rehab. He lived in Philadelphia until his death in 1967. John Coltrane's former home at **1511 North 33rd Street** is a National Historic Landmark.

Grace Kelly (1929-1982)

The cool beauty who starred in three Hitchcock movies was the daughter of triple Olympic champion John Brendan Kelly Sr. (⚫ p. 14). She grew up in Philadelphia before graduating high school and moving to New York where she landed a Broadway role. She became an international star in films such as *Rear Window* (1954), *High Noon* (1952), and *Mogambo* (1953).

In 1956, she married Prince Rainier of Monaco. You can see her childhood home in **East Falls**, a district in the northwest of Philadelphia.

Wilt Chamberlain (1936-1999)

Born in Philadelphia, this basketball player who stood 7ft 1in tall is regarded as one of the top 10 players in the history of the National Basketball Association (NBA). He played with the Philadelphia Warriors from 1959 to 1962 and the Philadelphia 76ers from 1965 to 1968. An outstanding athlete and excellent runner on court and jump-shooter, he had such power, agility, and speed that the NBA were forced to change certain basketball rules to overcome this superior defensive force. He's famed for popularizing the "slam dunk" (when a player jumps in the air and forces the ball through the basket) and perfecting the "finger roll". Chamberlain holds over 70 NBA records, including the highest number of points in a match, with 100 points.

Joe Frazier (1944-2011)

Hailed as one of the greatest professional boxers of all time, "Smokin' Joe" was the undisputed world heavyweight champion from 1970 to 1973 and won a gold medal at the 1964 Summer Olympics. Frazier is above all known for his matches against Mohamed Ali, who he fought and defeated on March 8, 1971, in the "fight of the century".

A. Alon/Alamy/hemis.fr

Wilt Chamberlain (1936-1999).

Patti LaBelle (1944)

Undoubtedly the most famous doyenne of **The Sound of Philadelphia** (*C p. 135*)**.** In the 1970s, Patti and her group released *Lady Marmalade,* a global hit and ranked on *Rolling Stone's* **list of The 500 Greatest Songs of All Time.** Patti LaBelle has during her seven-decade career sold over 50 million records and **won two Grammy Awards.**

Kevin Bacon (1958)

The youngest of six, Kevin is the son of the late Edmund Norwood Bacon, an eminent urban planner and architect from Philadelphia. In 1974, aged 16, he enrolled on the summer program of the Pennsylvania Governor's School for the Arts and studied theater. He left the family home at the age of 17 to start his acting career in New York. With over 90 films to his credit, the actor is best known for his roles in *Footloose* (1984), *JFK* (1991), *A Few Good Men* (1992), and *Mystic River* (2003). In 2004, Kevin Bacon returned to Philadelphia to film *The Woodsman.* Besides being a fine actor, Bacon is a musician; he and his older brother Michael formed the rock band Bacon Brothers.

Will Smith (1968)

Born in West Philadelphia, Will Smith first came to attention as a talented rapper, releasing hits including *Parents Just Don't Understand* and *Summertime.* He discovered his acting chops on *The Fresh Prince of Bel-Air,* in which he had the titular role. He achieved global fame for roles in blockbusters including *Bad Boys* (1995), *Independence Day* (1996), *Men in Black* (1997)... His performance in the lead role in *Ali* earned him an Oscar nomination in 2001. Will Smith has also played alongside his son Jaden in *After Earth* (2013), parts of which were shot in Philadelphia. He took home the Oscar for Best Actor in 2022 for his role in *King Richard*.

Foodie Philly

A Mid-Atlantic Melting Pot

Every culture has the keys to the city in Philadelphia. Visitors can snack on hot dogs with mustard from a street cart, smoked salmon bagels from a Jewish deli, dim sum at a family-run Chinese restaurant in Chinatown (*Addresses, p. 79*), and perhaps the best tacos in the U.S. (*Addresses, p. 81*).

Crab is king of the coast, and a host of restaurants serve up crab cakes, pan- or deep-fried. **Seafood** is available in all its forms: clams, mussels, shrimps, and oysters served raw, steamed, fried, or baked. Clam chowder is a New England specialty served in many local restaurants.

In Lancaster Country, **German culinary traditions**, perpetuated by the **Amish** community, have inspired many a robust dish: *Schnitz and Knepp* (ham or pork shoulder with dried apples and dumplings), *chowchow* (pickled cabbage, beans, peppers, and corn), *shoofly pie* (molasses and brown sugar in a flaky pie crust), *schnitz pie*, apple pie the Pennsylvanian Dutch way, and plenty of other desserts made with rhubarb, blueberries, and pecans. Sample a selection of these German specialties at **Reading Terminal Market** (*p. 42*), where you can also pick up foods from Amish farms. Brandywine Valley grows around 60% of the country's **mushrooms** and lots of local restaurants honor the humble fungus in a plethora of tasty dishes.

From Cheesesteaks to the Top Tables on the East Coast

It would be a culinary crime to overlook Philadelphia's famous specialty: the **cheesesteak**, a beefsteak and melted cheese sandwich invented, who would have bet, by the Italians (*Addresses, p. 75 and 76*). But Philly is far more than its eponymous sandwich, being home to some of the best chefs on the East Coast, including three winners of the prestigious **James Beard Award** (*Addresses, p. 81*), and countless inventive fine-dining establishments.

Farm to Table

Philadelphia leads the way in the **farm-to-table** movement. What's the idea? Giving diners the opportunity to enjoy local, healthy, organic fare. Some restaurants share the provenance of some ingredients used by their chef on their menu. Many will have come from the city's **Farmers' Markets**, where chefs routinely go to stock up their larders (*p. 94 and 97*).

And you can even eat well out and about: many **health-conscious** addresses serve beautifully fresh and seasonal salads along with freshly pressed fruit and vegetable juices.

Independence was declared here.
So, come enjoy whatever you want.

From cheesesteaks to music to world-class art, history, and retail, Philadelphia International Airport evokes and opens the door to everything this great city has to offer. See more at PHL.org.

PHL PHILADELPHIA INTERNATIONAL AIRPORT

INDEX

Symbols in the guide

★★★ Worth a special journey ★★ Worth a detour ★ Worth a visit

Hotels and Restaurants

9 rms	Number of rooms
bc	Beverage menu included
cc	Payment by credit card
⌿	Credit cards not accepted
	Air conditioning in room
✗	Restaurant in hotel
♀	Alcohol served
⌐	Swimming pool

Symbols

	Wi-Fi
⊙	Also see
⚲	Disabled Access
	A bit of advice / consider
♥	Recommended
A2 B	Map coordinates

Maps and Plans

MONUMENTS AND SITES

→	Sightseeing route
	Church
	Temple
	Synagogue
	Mosque
	Building - Tower
	Covered market
	Fort
	Castle
	Cave
	Fountain - Swamp
	Rampart - Gate

INFORMATION

	Tourist information
P PR	Parking - Park-and-Ride
	Tramway line
M ⓜ O	Underground - Tramway
	Railway Station - Bus Station
✈	Airport
	Cable car
	Funicular
	Tourist train
	City Hall - Post office
	Viewpoint - Panorama
	Ferry service: cars & passengers
	Ferry service: passengers only
B	Ferry over river : cars & passengers

MAJOR THOROUGHFARE, ROADS

	Motorway (unclassified)
	Tunnel
	Street - Road
	Pedestrian street
	Footpath, Trail

SPORTS AND RECREATION

	Swimming pool : open air, covered
	Horse racetrack
	Cycling path
	Stadium
	Beach
	Marina

THE COUNTRYSIDE
OF PHILADELPHIA

Just beyond the bustle of the city,
around the curve of the river and into lush rolling hills,
lies The Countryside of Philadelphia.

Valley Forge Casino Resort

King of Prussia Mall

Tax-free shopping on all clothing & shoes

Longwood Gardens

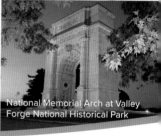

National Memorial Arch at Valley Forge National Historical Park

The Countryside of Philadelphia is conveniently located on the East Coast between New York City and Washington, D.C. and just minutes from Philadelphia. Close to Philadelphia International Airport and accessible by rail and all major roadways, The Countryside is a great addition to any east coast itinerary.

COUNTRYSIDEPHL.COM

Collection managed by Philippe Orain

Editorial Director	Éric Boucher
Editorial Secretary	Émilie Vialettes
Editors	Nora Gherras, Éric Boucher
Translator	LanguageWire
Contributors	Dănut-Marian Ţucă, Denis Rasse, Costina-Ionela Lungu, Theodor Cepraga (**Cartography**), Véronique Aissani, Carole Diascorn (**Cover**), Marion Capera, Marie Simonet (**Picture Editors**), Andra-Florentina Ostafi (**Objective Data**), Bogdan Gheorghiu, Cristian Catona, Hervé Dubois, Pascal Grougon (**Prepress**), Dominique Auclair (**Production Manager**)
	Maps : © MICHELIN 2023
Acknowledgments	**Philadelphia Convention & Visitors Bureau**: Robin Bloom, Director of Content; John Ryan, Social Media Specialist; Melissa McClure, Global Tourism Sales Manager; Svetlana Yazovskikh, Vice President of Global Tourism
Graphic Design	Laurent Muller (interior layout)
	Véronique Aissani (cover)
Advertising Sales and Partnerships	contact.clients@editions.michelin.com
	The content of any advertising pages contained in this guide is the sole responsibility of advertisers.
Contacts	Your opinion is essential to improving our products
	Help us by answering the questionnaire on our website:
	editions.michelin.com

Published in 2023

MICHELIN Éditions

A French stock company with capital of 487,500 euro
57 rue Gaston Tessier – 75019 Paris (France)
Registered in Paris: 882 639 354

© 2023 MICHELIN Éditions - All rights reserved
Registration of Copyright: 03-2023 – ISSN 0293-9436
Typography/Photoengraving: MICHELIN Éditions Paris
Printer: Estimprim, France
Printed in France: 03-2023

Facility 14001 certified
Printed on sustainably sourced paper

Photo credits p. 4-5
(left to right and top to bottom)

Jeff Fusco PHLCVB
Kyle Huff PHLCVB
Kyle Huff PHLCVB
Kyle Huff PHLCVB
Kyle Huff PHLCVB
f11photo Getty Images Plus
Ethan Shaw Getty Images Plus
zrfphoto Getty Images Plus
miralex Getty Images Plus
Mira/Alamy/hemis.fr